OFFICIAL SQA PAST PAPERS WITH ANSWERS

HIGHER

ENGLISH
2006-2009

First exam published in 2006.

Published by Bright Red Publishing Ltd, 6 Stafford Street, Edinburgh EH3 7AU

tel: 0131 220 5804 fax: 0131 220 6710 info@brightredpublishing.co.uk www.brightredpublishing.co.uk

ISBN 978-1-84948-057-4

A CIP Catalogue record for this book is available from the British Library.

Bright Red Publishing is grateful to the copyright holders, as credited on the final page of the book, for permission to use their material. Every effort has been made to trace the copyright holders and to obtain their permission for the use of copyright material. Bright Red Publishing will be happy to receive information allowing us to rectify any error or omission in future editions.

2006

[BLANK PAGE]

X115/301

NATIONAL QUALIFICATIONS 2006	FRIDAY, 12 MAY 9.00 AM – 10.30 AM	**ENGLISH** HIGHER Close Reading—Text

There are TWO passages and questions.

Read the passages carefully and then answer all the questions, which are printed in a separate booklet.

You should read the passages to:

understand what the writers are saying about problems of diet and obesity in the modern world (**Understanding—U**);

analyse their choices of language, imagery and structures to recognise how they convey their points of view and contribute to the impact of the passage (**Analysis—A**);

evaluate how effectively they have achieved their purpose (**Evaluation—E**).

SCOTTISH
QUALIFICATIONS
AUTHORITY

    ©

PASSAGE 1

The first passage is from an article in The Economist *magazine in December 2003. In it, the writer explores the problem of obesity in the modern world.*

THE SHAPE OF THINGS TO COME

When the world was a simpler place, the rich were fat, the poor were thin, and right-thinking people worried about how to feed the hungry. Now, in much of 5 the world, the rich are thin, the poor are fat, and right-thinking people are worrying about obesity.

Evolution is mostly to blame. It has designed mankind to cope with 10 deprivation, not plenty. People are perfectly tuned to store energy in good years to see them through lean ones. But when bad times never come, they are stuck with that energy, stored around 15 their expanding bellies.

Thanks to rising agricultural productivity, lean years are rarer all over the globe. Pessimistic economists, who used to draw graphs proving that the 20 world was shortly going to run out of food, have gone rather quiet lately. According to the UN, the number of people short of food fell from 920m in 1980 to 799m 20 years later, even though 25 the world's population increased by 1·6 billion over the period. This is mostly a cause for celebration. Mankind has won what was, for most of his time on this planet, his biggest battle: to ensure that 30 he and his offspring had enough to eat. But every silver lining has a cloud, and the consequence of prosperity is a new plague that brings with it a host of interesting policy dilemmas.

35 There is no doubt that obesity is the world's biggest public-health issue today—the main cause of heart disease, which kills more people these days than AIDS, malaria, war; the principal risk factor in diabetes; heavily implicated in 40 cancer and other diseases. Since the World Health Organisation labelled obesity an epidemic in 2000, reports on its fearful consequences have come thick and fast. 45

Will public-health warnings, combined with media pressure, persuade people to get thinner, just as such warnings finally put them off tobacco? Possibly. In the rich world, sales of healthier foods are 50 booming and new figures suggest that over the past year Americans got very slightly thinner for the first time in recorded history. But even if Americans are losing a few ounces, it will be many 55 years before their country solves the health problems caused by half a century's dining to excess. And everywhere else in the economically developed world, people are still piling 60 on the pounds.

That's why there is now a worldwide consensus among doctors that governments should do something to stop them. There's nothing radical about 65 the idea that governments should intervene in the food business. They've been at it since 1202, when King John of England first banned the adulteration of bread. Governments and the public 70 seem to agree that ensuring the safety and stability of the food supply is part of the state's job. But obesity is a more complicated issue than food safety. It is not about ensuring that people don't get 75 poisoned: it is about changing their behaviour.

Should governments be trying to do anything about it at all?

80 There is one bad reason for doing something, and two good reasons. The bad reason is that governments should help citizens look after themselves. People, the argument goes, are misled by
85 their genes, which are constantly trying to pack away a few more calories just in case of a famine around the corner. Governments should help guide them towards better eating habits. But that
90 argument is weaker in the case of food than it is for tobacco—nicotine is addictive, chocolate is not—and no better than it is in any other area where people have a choice of being sensible or
95 silly. People are constantly torn by the battle between their better and worse selves. It's up to them, not governments, to decide who should win.

A better argument for intervention is
100 that dietary habits are established early in childhood. Once people get fat, it is hard for them to get thin; once they are used to breakfasting on chips and fizzy drinks, that's hard to change. The state, which
105 has some responsibility for moulding minors, should try to ensure that its small citizens aren't mainlining sugar at primary school. Britain's government is gesturing towards tough restrictions on
110 advertising junk food to children. That seems unlikely to have much effect. Sweden already bans advertising to children, and its young people are as porky as those in comparable countries. Other moves, such as banning junk food 115 from schools, might work better. In some countries, such as America, soft-drinks companies bribe schools to let them install vending machines. That should stop. 120

A second plausible argument for intervention is that thin people subsidise fat people through contributions to the National Health Service. If everybody is forced to carry the weight of the seriously 125 fat, then everybody has an interest in seeing them slim down. That is why some people believe the government should tax fattening food—sweets, snacks and take-aways. They argue this 130 might discourage consumption of unhealthy food and recoup some of the costs of obesity.

It might; but it would also constitute too great an intrusion on liberty for the gain 135 in equity and efficiency it might (or might not) represent. Society has a legitimate interest in fat, because fat and thin people both pay for it. But it also has a legitimate interest in not having the 140 government stick its nose too far into the private sphere. If people want to eat their way to grossness and an early grave, let them.

[Turn over

PASSAGE 2

The second passage appeared as an article in The Observer *newspaper in May 2004. In it, Susie Orbach, a clinician who has worked for many years with people suffering from eating problems, suggests that there are different views on the "obesity epidemic".*

FOOLISH PANIC IS ABOUT PROFIT

At primary school, my son's lunch-box was inspected and found to fail. It contained chocolate biscuits. The school, believing it was doing the right
5 thing, had banned sweets, chocolates and crisps in the name of good nutrition.

After school and in the playground, away from the teachers' eyes, sweets and chocolates were traded. They became
10 the marks of rebellion and the statements of independence. Eating foods they suspected the grown-ups would rather they didn't, made those foods ever so much more enticing. They
15 weren't just food but food plus attitude.

The school was well-meaning—just misguided. Its attitude, like most of what permeates the obesity debate, has turned good intentions into
20 bad conclusions. Despite endless thoughtful discussion on the subject, we are left with a sense that obesity is about to destabilise the NHS, that dangerous fat is swamping the nation.

25 That there is a considerable increase in obesity is not in question. The extent of it is. For many, obesity is a source of anguish and severe health difficulties. But the motivation of some of those who
30 trumpet these dangers associated with obesity needs to be questioned. There is considerable evidence that there is serious money to be made from a condition in search of treatment, and
35 the categorisation of fat may just fit this bill perfectly. In the US, commercial slimming clubs and similar groups contributed millions of dollars to Shape Up America, an organisation which was
40 part of a strategy to turn obesity into a disease which can be treated by the pharmaceutical, diet and medical industries. Medicine is, after all, an industry in the US.

So sections of the market aim to profit 45 from the notion that we are all too fat. We need to contest that. It isn't the case. Evidence from the professional journals shows that fitness, not fat, determines our mortality. You can be 50 fat, fit and healthy.

We are in danger of being too willing to mimic the US dogma on the demonisation of fat and of particular foods. This matters because it creates a 55 climate in which the government may fail to ask fundamental questions about whose interests are served by the introduction of hysteria around obesity; particularly who profits and who hurts. 60 A corrective to the scare tactics is needed. People should consider, for example, the simple fact that the new rise in obesity is not simple growth, but is partly due to the body mass index 65 (BMI) being revised downwards in the past six years. If you are Brad Pitt, you are now considered overweight. If you are as substantial as Russell Crowe, you are obese. Overnight 36 million 70 Americans woke up to find that they were obese.

The hidden psychological effects of this attack on our body size are enormous. We are not going to protect the next 75 generation by simply exhorting them to eat so-called good foods.

There is a lot to be done. We need to address what food means in people's emotional lives. We need to transform 80 the culture of thinness. We need to recognise that we as a society are deeply confused about eating and dieting. And we need to realise that part of this confusion has been cynically promoted 85 by those who now are selling us the obesity epidemic.

[END OF TEXT]

X115/302

NATIONAL
QUALIFICATIONS
2006

FRIDAY, 12 MAY
9.00 AM – 10.30 AM

ENGLISH
HIGHER
Close Reading–Questions

Answer all questions. **Use your own words whenever possible and particularly when you are instructed to do so.**

50 marks are allocated to this paper.

A code letter (U, A, E) is used alongside each question to give some indication of the skills being assessed. The number of marks attached to each question will give some indication of the length of answer required.

SCOTTISH
QUALIFICATIONS
AUTHORITY

Questions on Passage 1

Marks *Code*

1. Read the first paragraph (lines 1–7).

    (a) Explain briefly how the concerns of "right-thinking people" have changed over time.   1   U

    (b) Identify **two** ways by which the sentence structure in these lines emphasises the change.   2   A

2. "Evolution is mostly to blame." (line 8)

    How does the writer go on to explain this statement? You should refer to lines 8–15 and use your own words as far as possible.   2   U

3. Read lines 16–34.

    (a) Why, according to lines 16–26, have the "pessimistic economists . . . gone rather quiet"?   1   U

    (b) "This is mostly a cause for celebration." (lines 26–27)

    What evidence does the writer provide in lines 27–34 to support this statement?   2   U

    (c) How effective do you find the imagery of lines 27–34 in illustrating the writer's line of thought? You must refer to **two** examples in your answer.   4   A/E

4. How does the writer's language in lines 35–45 stress the seriousness of the health problem?

    In your answer you should refer to at least two features such as sentence structure, word choice, tone . . .   4   A

5. Identify from lines 46–61 one cause for hope and one cause for concern. Use your own words as far as possible.   2   U

6. In lines 62–133 the writer moves on to discuss the arguments for and against government intervention in the food industry.

    (a) According to lines 62–77, what was the purpose of government intervention in the past, and what is a further purpose of its intervention now?   2   U

    (b) Read carefully lines 80–133.

    Summarise the key points of the "one bad reason" and the "two good reasons" (lines 80–81) for government intervention in food policy. You must use your own words as far as possible.   6   U

7. In the final paragraph (lines 134–144) the writer makes clear that he disapproves of too much government intervention.

    Show how the writer uses particular features of language to demonstrate his strength of feeling.   4   A

                                                                                                                    (30)

ENGLISH HIGHER
CLOSE READING 2006

1. (a) a brief reference to the change from concern about (the effects of) too little food to concern about (the effects of) too much

(b) *Possible answers include*:
1. parallelism/balanced construction
2. series of contrasts ("when/now" … "fat/thin" … "feed the hungry/obesity")
3. repetition of "rich…poor…right-thinking"
4. two compound sentences with co-ordinate clauses in which the attributes are reversed

2. *Any two of the following*:
1. acceptable gloss on "has designed mankind"
2. humans have the ability to survive shortages by storing reserves
3. in a period of continuous prosperity people become increasingly bigger

3. (a) *Either of the following*:
1. they have been proved wrong
2. (although the population of the world has risen) the number of people who are hungry has fallen.

(b) "cause for celebration" there is now, according to the writer, sufficient food for mankind.
"mostly" the drawback is that we now have another problem.

(c) *Possible answers are*:
1. "won … battle"
idea of struggle, succeeding in a difficult situation
2. "offspring"
idea of product, source … importance of survival of the genetic line
3. "silver lining"
idea of shining/bright side, redeeming aspect of an otherwise unpleasant situation
4. "cloud"
dull or dark spot, sense of threat
5. "plague"
idea of deadly epidemic, potential devastation caused by problem
6. "host"
idea of large number, threat, army (and possible link to "won … battle").

4. *Possible answers are*:
Sentence structure:
1. generic statement/assertion (lines 35–37) appears to brook no argument
2. single dash
used to explain/exemplify the opening statement by introducing the main risk

3. semi-colons
used to separate items in a list which emphasises the serious/life-threatening consequences of obesity
4. listing
emphasises the number and/or cumulative effect of health-related problems
5. second sentence
provides a summation of the dire effects of obesity

Word choice:
6. "no doubt"
emphatic
7. "biggest"
use of superlative
8. "main cause"
idea of strength/power
9. "kills"
idea of deadly threat
10. "principal risk factor"
idea of statistical approach to danger
11. "heavily implicated"
idea of blame
12. "labelled"
idea of superficiality, pejorative tag
13. "epidemic"
idea of a disease out of control
14. "fearful consequences"
idea of a frightening, menacing future
15. "thick and fast"
idea that the extent/volume/speed of the reaction is almost out of control

Tone:
16. any acceptable suggestion, e.g. relentlessly serious, slightly melodramatic, possibly ironic… – supported by appropriate reference and explanation

5. Cause for hope
Any one of the following:
1. gloss on "public health warnings" and "media pressure"
2. reduction in smoking
3. increase in sale of health foods
4. (slight) reduction in weight of Americans

Cause for concern
Either of the following:
5. it will require a lengthy period of time for people to shed so much excess weight
6. meanwhile, there is an increase in weight throughout the more prosperous parts of the world.

6. (*a*) In the past: to assure quality of food/make food safer/guarantee regular availability of food.
Now: gloss on "changing their behaviour", eg to transform eating habits.

(*b*) "bad reason" (lines 80–98):
The crux of the paragraph is in lines 89–98 ("But …"). ie the writer's objections in terms of the "nanny state", intrusion into personal freedom, discouragement of personal responsibility, etc.
"first good reason" (lines 99–120):
The crux of the paragraph is the government's role in the protection of children, who are vulnerable/at risk for biological and/or social and/or commercial reasons.
"second good reason" (lines 121–133):
The crux is in the financial argument about the "unfairness"/imbalance in terms of contributions to and burdens upon the NHS.

7. *Possible answers are*:
Sentence structure:
1. bluntness of opening "It might"
2. parenthesis for "(or might not)" – throwaway remark
3. use of "But" at start of sentence – clear indication of contradiction to come
4. repetition of "legitimate interest" – rhetorical device to squash his earlier case
5. delayed "let them" at end of paragraph – dismissive

Word choice:
6. formality of word choice ("constitute … intrusion on liberty … gain in equity and efficiency … legitimate interest") – bombastic, legalistic overtones.
7. informality of word choice ("stick its nose … grossness … early grave") – blunt, direct

Tone:
8. contemptuous - informality/vulgarity of "stick its nose … grossness … early grave"
9. elevated, rather hectoring – "constitute … intrusion on liberty … private sphere"

Contrast:
10. contrast in register and/or tone (see 6, 7, 8 and 9 above)

Sound:
11. alliteration in "grossness … grave" – harsh, contemptuous

8. (*a*) Answers should show an understanding of "well-meaning" and of "misguided" and imply the contradiction, eg: The school thought it was healthy to ban sweets, but they caused the sweets to become even more attractive in the pupils' eyes.

(*b*) The attitude – one of defiance/rebellion/anti-authoritarianism – will be implied.
Possible answers are:
1. "(away from the) teachers' eyes"
suggests avoidance of authority of the all seeing classroom eye

2. "traded"
suggests an illicit, appealing bargaining
3. "(marks of) rebellion"
exaggerates the significance of the swapping, but leaves the idea of the anti-authoritarian behaviour
4. "(statements of) independence"
suggests the dawning awakening of action not sanctioned by authority
5. "suspected"/"rather they didn't"
suggests a confused delight in thwarting the wishes of adults
6. "ever so much more"
suggests the excessive importance placed on a few relatively unimportant sweets
7. "enticing"
suggests the illicit, forbidden fruit idea
8. "not just food but"
suggests that the sweets had become an anti-authoritarian symbol
9. "food plus attitude"
suggests the sweets acquired a significance in the adoption of a stance against authority which soared beyond their importance as sweets.

9. Motivation:
money-making/
financial advantage/economic growth.
Illustrated by:
Those who are likely to make money (e.g. slimming clubs, chemists, doctors, campaigning organisations) will make it sound like an illness so they can be paid to treat it.

10. *Possible answers are*:
1. "So…"
introduces a sentence which sums up the argument so far
2. the use of short sentences
gives each idea an importance of its own for us to digest and recognise; sense of stating simple indisputable fact
3. "fitness, not fat, …"
the balance/contrast is highlighted by the separation by commas or by the alliteration
4. "You…"
direct address, inclusive lead-in to final point
5. the list in the last sentence
short, punchy, climactic; helps us to reach an easily understood conclusion

11. (*a*) *Possible answers are*:
Word choice/imagery:
1. "danger"
suggestion of threat
2. "mimic"
suggestion of unthinking acceptance
3. "dogma"
suggestion of irrational, unbending, obstructive views
4. "demonisation"
suggestion of threat from evil forces, a satanic process

5. "hysteria"
suggestion of irrational fears being exploited

Sentence structure:

6. "who profits and who hurts"
summing up, simplifying the argument,
bringing it to a head and emphasising "hurts"

7. climax (after pause created by semicolon) as for
point 6

Tone:

8. any sensible suggestion such as scathing, critical,
dogmatic, hectoring ... – supported by
appropriate reference and explanation.

(*b*) Answers should show a clear understanding that the
"corrective" is for us to be aware of the distorting
effects of the alteration to the BMI – that it makes
the numbers of obese people seem greater or that it
has caused quite ordinary-sized people to be classed
as obese/overweight.

12. *Possible answers are*:

Sentence structure:

1. short sentence - "There is a lot to be done" sets up
an unmistakable agenda which acts as the topic for
the rest of the paragraph

2. repetition of "We need"
harps on the necessity for doing something, sets up
a badgering, hectoring tone

3. use of "And" to begin the final sentence
by separating the final point into a distinct sentence
we focus on who should be blamed for this
confusion – the commercial interests

4. climactic nature of the paragraph
repetition of "We need" followed by the final "And
we need" sets up a climax which is also emphasised
by the use of short sentences followed by longer
ones making us focus on the exploitative industries.

Word choice:

5. "emotional lives"
the idea that we are too captive to our feelings

6. "transform"
the change needs to be more than minor –
transformation suggests a profound and far-
reaching change

7. "culture (of thinness)"
suggests that thinness as an ideal has become deeply
embedded in the way of life and assumptions of
society

8. "deeply (confused)"
the problems are profound and will need a huge
effort to eradicate them

9. "cynically (promoted)"
our anxieties are being exploited for gain

10. "selling (us)"
suggests that there needs to be a salesman who will
exaggerate the problems associated with the idea of
obesity

11. "(obesity) epidemic"
suggests that the situation is out of control like an
infectious disease which cannot be stopped

Tone:

12. any sensible suggestion such as hectoring, pleading,
impatient ... – supported by appropriate reference
and explanation, probably to one or more of 1-11
above

13. (*a*) *Passage 1*:   obesity is the greatest danger, a major
danger, a serious problem ...

      Passage 2:   obesity is not such a big problem as
is being suggested and/or people are
making money from exaggerating the
problem

NB: The difference may be established implicitly,
e.g. "Passage 2 thinks obesity is not a big problem".

(*b*) Note that the question asks for concentration on
style of writing, although there is reference to the
"opening stages of an argument". Implicit
understanding of each writer's point of view will
certainly be a feature of good answers. A succinct,
sophisticated response will be worth more than a
series of fairly trivial points and obvious references.
For full marks, there must be reference to both
passages (although not necessarily a balanced
treatment) and convincing evaluative comment.

Try to focus on the **presentation/introduction** of
the ideas and not on the ideas themselves
Any of the points below would be valid comment:

Passage 1:

• the wordplay in paragraph 1, use of repetition,
parallelism

• the short sentence to highlight main cause:
evolution

• word choice such as "expanding bellies", "fearful
consequences" ...

• the use of statistics/selection of dramatic, serious
illnesses

• imagery such as "battle", "plague" ...

• wordplay in "every silver lining has a cloud" ...

• climactic nature of sentence structure (lines 35-
45)

Passage 2:

• the nature of the introductory anecdote/human
interest story

• word choice such as "food plus attitude",
"swamping", "trumpet", "serious money" ...

• exaggeration such as "endless", "destabilise",
"swamping", "millions" ...

• language of business/money such as
"commercial", "industry", "market", "profit" ...

• sentence structure of lines 45-51

ENGLISH HIGHER
CRITICAL ESSAY 2006

Please see the Critical Essay guidelines for the English Higher 2009 on page 22.

ENGLISH HIGHER
CLOSE READING 2007

Questions on Passage 1

1. (a) Acceptable gloss on "ecstatic" - e.g. joyous, thrilled, excited, delighted ...; "happy" by itself is not acceptable: there must be some idea of intensity

   Acceptable gloss on "nostalgic" - e.g. looking back fondly, wistful, regretful, reflective, ... "sad/unhappy" by itself not acceptable - there must be some idea of something connected with past OR the idea that he is apprehensive, fearful (at possible loss/demise of libraries)

   (b) *Possible answers are*:
   1. "book-lined" suggests large number/area of books, implying organised, impressive nature...
   2. "cathedral-quiet" has connotations of solemnity, reverence, devotion, large hushed space...
   3. "cherished" suggests cared for emotionally (rather than just practically), warmth...
   4. "civilisation" has connotations of that which marks us out from less sophisticated societies
   5. "lose" has a sense of being deprived, bereft...
   6. "cultural" suggests traditions, heritage, civilised society,...
   7. "peril" suggests threat, risk, menace, danger (to something precious)

2. *Possible answers are*:

   "High priority":
   1. use of "remembered" suggests that the library, although initially overlooked, was indeed a priority.
   2. despite the fact they "neglected shops and amenities", they still put in a library, which suggests that it was considered more important than these.

   "Low priority":
   3. the high number (60,000) of potential users contrasted with the smallness of the facility (a "shed") suggests inadequacy.
   4. use of "remembered" suggests it was an afterthought, a last-minute idea.
   5. the fact it was a "wooden shed" suggests it was basic, cheap, unsophisticated, temporary and therefore considered of little importance.
   6. the use of "somehow" indicates that nobody was sure why the decision had been taken; it just happened.
   7. the tone of "- actually, a wooden shed" as if a rather amused, sarcastic aside suggests an afterthought, a wry admission of its inadequacies.

3. *Possible answers*:

   Imagery:
   1. "stretching"
      gives the impression of something being pulled or elongated with connotations of never-ending, upward movement, aspiring

2. "cocooned":
as larvae are protected and self-contained in their cocoons, so each floor in the library is separate and shelters the students within their specialised knowledge areas

3. "worlds of knowledge"
the number of floors is so great and they are so separate that they are like different, independent planetary systems, each specialising in a particular area of knowledge

4. "planets"
the separation into large, distinct learning areas, each self-contained like the isolation and individualism of each planet in space

Word choice:

5. "wonder"
connotations of awe, freshness, childlike amazement, admiration …

6. "skyscraper (library)"
slightly exaggerated description suggests size and magnificence (be sympathetic to candidates who choose to see "skyscraper" as an image)

7. "vast"
gives the impression of an enormous extent of space

8. "atrium"
idea of large, impressive central area – with connotations of classical ideas/learning

9. "devoted"
connotations of love, reverence, dedication …

10. "chatting, flirting, doodling, panicking"
(any of these) - suggestions of human foibles, ordinary behaviour contrasted with the extraordinary nature of the library

11. "exploring"
suggests excitement of new discovery, sense of quest, hint of size,…

12. "unique"
suggestions of something very special, to be marvelled at …

N.B. words from 1–4 above could be the subject of appropriate comments as word choice.

4. (a) *Possible answers are*:

Sentence structure:

1. the climactic nature of the second sentence: building up from an abrupt start to the negative attitude by "chatter…at a thousand decibels" **or** (possibly) presents a positive attitude in admiring their ability to communicate loudly or their ability to carry out more than one task at a time.

2. use of questions: could suggest a positive attitude by backing up the idea that young people are modern and that they do not approve of subsidising libraries **or** combined with a mock-scornful tone could suggest that he believes the answer to the questions is that we do need libraries rather than the slick media world of the MTV generation – ie a negative attitude.

3. structure of the first sentence: a case might just be made that the colon is used to introduce a

demonstration of the writer's attitude that he prefers the past to the present and therefore will be critical of the MTV generation.

Word choice:

4. "multi-tasking": suggests positive attitude in that these people are seen as talented in their ability to perform several tasks simultaneously **or** suggests a negative attitude in that in trying to do so many things at once, due attention is not given to the important matters.

5. "cheap books": suggests positive aspects in that these books are readily available to all without recourse to a library **or** negatively, the books are cheap in the sense of not worth much intellectually.

6. "chatter": negative in that the word suggests inconsequential communication **or** positive in that it suggests easy personal interaction.

7. "thousand decibels": probably negative in that it suggests that the noise is too loud for real thought.

8. "old-fashioned": probably negative in that it suggests he thinks the MTV generation is too readily dismissive, or too keen to believe libraries are outdated.

Tone:

9. derogatory: (backed up by any of the comments suggested above)

10. admiring: (backed up by any of the comments suggested above)

11. mock-scornful/sarcastic: (backed up by any of the comments suggested above)

(b) A basic understanding that diminishing use of libraries leads to diminishing levels of provision, which leads to diminishing use …

5. (a) *Any four of the following*:

1. idea of accessibility (ie acceptable gloss on "strategically situated")

2. idea of free access (ie acceptable gloss on "too expensive … to buy")

3. idea that resources are more sophisticated (ie acceptable gloss on "too complex to find online")

4. idea of supporting democratic responsibilities (ie acceptable gloss on "informed citizenship")

5. idea of community awareness/cohesion (ie acceptable gloss on "civic pride")

6. idea of professional support (ie acceptable gloss on "trained librarian")

7. idea of informed/refined selection (ie acceptable gloss on "honed and developed by experts")

8. idea of high standard of material (ie acceptable gloss on "quality … of information")

9. idea of authenticity (ie acceptable gloss on "veracity of information")

10. idea of selectivity of information (in contrast with junk online)

(b) For libraries, answers should make acceptable comment on the positive connotations of any of the

following:
"trained"
"honed"
"developed"
"experts"
"guarantee"
"quality"
"veracity"
For the internet, answers should make acceptable comment on the negative connotations of any of the following:
"Achilles' heel"
"(of course) nonsense"
"cluttered"
"false"
"(plain) junk"
"never"

6. (a) any acceptable gloss, e.g. guardians, protectors, those who keep something safe, ...

(b) *Possible answers are*:

Word choice:
1. "(become the) fashion": connotations of transience, shallowness, ...
2. "entertainment centres"/"audio-visuals": connotations of pandering to popular taste, lack of seriousness, ...
3. "gimmicks": connotations of cheap trickery, merely to capture attention, ...
4. "popularising": connotations of dumbing down, aiming for lowest common denominator, ...
5. "reduced": connotations of loss of quality, depth, sophistication, ...
6. "child's view": connotations of naiveté, lack of sophistication, limited perspective, ...

Tone:
7. grudging: "some (enthusiasm)" suggests reluctance to welcome the idea fully
8. scornful: appropriate comment based on any of 1–6 above
9. didactic: appropriate comment on lines 52–54 ("cannot always be reduced", "duty", "future generations", "invest", "culture")

Structure:
10. list ("audio-visuals, interactive displays and gimmicks"), ending in the anti-climax ("gimmicks"): reduces the other items to meaningless technical tricks.
11. structure of "While I have ... universe" is a limited concession which emphasises the dismissiveness of what follows.

7. *Possible answers are*:

Ideas:
1. Google and the Bodleian Library are brought together again in this paragraph.
2. The idea of large numbers (one million books) on Google/the vastness of libraries leading to an understanding of the enormous amount of material which can never be known.

3. The differentiation between information and wisdom is what the passage has been leading up to.

Language:
4. "Of course": strategic concession/ idea of bringing reader onside/of being reasonable – in preparation for conclusion.
5. "Yet here's": conversational tone leads the reader to come on board and share his ideas.
6. "daunting": strong word suggesting the enormous and frightening amount of knowledge.
7. "even a fraction": suggests, in contrast, the very small proportion with which one person can come to grips.
8. "Ever.": emphatic, one word sentence closes the door on the possibility of conquering all knowledge.
9. "merely imbibing": in contrast with wisdom, this suggests that information acquired simply as quantity, without understanding or context, is as mechanical as drinking.
10. word order in last sentence: the inversion of normal order places the realisation very close to the "ever" which gives it more impact, and leaves the important word "wisdom" to follow its verb and take a central place in the last sentence
11. dash plus final statement in last sentence: the pause created by the dash puts emphasis on the last words ("merely imbibing information"), throwing them into stronger contrast with "the beginning of wisdom" which is the thrust of the passage as a whole.

Questions on Passage 2

8. (a) *Any one of the following*:
1. (very) happy
2. idyllic
3. carefree
4. nostalgic
5. calm, peaceful
6. any other answer which conveys a positive feeling or the importance of the memory to the writer

(b) *Possible answers are*:
1. "We are surrounded by eight million books.": The very short, declarative, unembellished sentence emphasises the simple, breathtaking fact.
2. "eight million books": overwhelming sense of quantity.
3. "on every side": awe-inspiring because books are inescapable, almost intimidating.
4. "hundreds of yards deep": the sheer scale of the collection.
5. "at the rate of two miles a year": impressive growth rate.
6. "surrounded by", "Behind", "beneath": directional details - use of a variety of

prepositions and adverbial phrases of place convey the omnipresence of books.

7. "reach into the sky": idea of towering beyond the normal, aspirational, connotations of heavenly, …

8. "(in compact) ranks" image of armed forces which suggests the highly organised positioning of the books.

9. "subterranean": sense of dark, mysterious, alluring.

10. "subterranean stacks": alliteration suggests hushed reverence.

11. "entombed in words": image of burial suggests the all-encompassing presence of books.

12. "unimaginable (volume)": beyond the power of the mind to conceive

13. "cold storage": sci-fi idea of some potential waiting to be revived.

14. "quiet and vast and waiting": climactic description suggests the overpowering, slightly menacing, nature of such an enormous collection.

(c) *Possible answer*:

The repetition of "perhaps" conveys the writer's wistful uncertainty and makes the reader aware that he has a wealth of happy memories from which to choose.

9. Possible comments:

1. "temple": just as a temple is a place of worship and reverence, a library deserves our utmost respect (because of the accumulation of knowledge which it contains).

2. "core": just as the core is the heart, the essential part, a library is central to our lives and society.

3. "citadel": just as a citadel is a fortress, a library provides a stronghold to safeguard all that we consider most precious.

10. (a) It could signal the end of conventional libraries, (which will no longer be used), ie a basic understanding of "could finally destroy traditional libraries, which will become mere warehouses for the physical objects, empty of people and life" (lines 28-30).

(b) *Any three of the following*:

1. a single catalogue will ensure that everything is stored in one place.

2. democracy – knowledge will be available to all.

3. it will be impossible to wipe out knowledge (by destroying books).

4. totalitarian states will not be able to keep knowledge to themselves/deny it to the masses.

11. (a) Marks will depend on the clarity of the explanation

Either or both of the following:

1. there is visual beauty in the book itself.

2. there is sensual pleasure in holding the actual book.

Marks will depend on the clarity of the explanation.

(b) *Any one or more of the following*:

1. acceptable gloss on "central to our understanding of what it is to be human" – libraries allow us to find out about life and our position in it

2. acceptable gloss on "sociable thinking, exploring and exchanging ideas" – function of libraries as a meeting place for discussion

3. acceptable gloss on "recreational" – libraries as places of relaxation or even romance

12. *Potential answers*:

Ideas:

1. the film illustrates the conflict between libraries and new technology - the two main characters represent the two sides

2. the passage ends on a positive note - libraries and online catalogue can happily co-exist

Language/Style:

3. literal and metaphorical marriage

4. "smooching" - jocular, informal reference to easy, affectionate, slightly old-fashioned relationship

5. play on words - "everyone reads happily ever after"

6. single sentence final paragraph sums up the link between the film and the co-existence of libraries and an online catalogue.

Questions on both Passages

13. The mark for this question will reflect the overall quality of the response and may not be directly related to the length of response or to the number of points/references made. A succinct, sophisticated response will be worth more than a series of fairly trivial points and obvious references.

For full marks there must be a reference to both elements (ie ideas and style) and to both passages (although not necessarily a balanced treatment) and convincing evaluative comment.

- Some candidates may choose to argue that the passages are equally persuasive, focusing in (part of) their answers on similarities in ideas, style and length. This could be a legitimate approach and such answers should be judged on their merits.

- Some candidates may make use of the writers' criticisms of the internet to imply support for libraries. This is broadly acceptable, provided it contributes effectively to a line of thought about the writers' views.

Any of the points below would be valid comment:

Ideas – Passage 1:

- libraries are a part of civilisation
- libraries aid learning
- libraries as a physical space can have an important/positive impact on people

13. *continued*

- libraries allow shared learning experiences
- libraries allow people to socialise
- libraries encourage people to explore other areas of knowledge
- libraries allow easy and affordable access to books/knowledge
- librarians offer vital expertise
- libraries are user-friendly
- (as opposed to the internet) people can have confidence in the authenticity/validity/reliability of material in libraries
- libraries safeguard important books/documents/materials
- libraries as a physical space emphasise the extent of human knowledge

Ideas – Passage 2:

- libraries encourage young people's interest in reading
- libraries are linked to civilised values
- libraries make the acquisition of knowledge a sociable activity
- libraries are symbolic representations of civilisation/knowledge/man's finer points
- libraries allow easy access to books as physical objects (which the writer thinks is important)
- people are reading more books than ever
- (however, libraries are vulnerable guardians of knowledge)

Style – Passage 1:

- use of varied personal memories as platform for ideas/observations
- detailed, evocative use of language to convey love of libraries
- variation in tone to match flow of argument (humorous, nostalgic, assertive, dismissive, conversational, etc)
- use of statistics
- forceful ending to stress importance of ideas

Style – Passage 2:

- use of varied personal memories as platform for ideas/observations
- use of sensual language to convey emotional nature of engagement
- use of various stylistic devices to convey his awe/reverence for libraries (facts and figures; extended imagery; accumulative style)
- use of historical perspective to contextualise the importance and evolving nature of libraries
- use of humour, especially in the rather playful ending

ENGLISH HIGHER CRITICAL ESSAY 2007

Please see the Critical Essay guidelines for the English Higher 2009 on page 22.

ENGLISH HIGHER
CLOSE READING 2008

1. 1. gloss on "one could be forgiven for thinking that we still live in small peasant communities dependent upon the minutest shift in agricultural policy" – idea that we are still a rural society affected by farming laws or

2. gloss on "it has seemed almost as if we were still in the early nineteenth century when we relied on the countryside to survive" – as if we were still living in the past when we were more rurally dependent

2. (a) *Possible answers*:

Word choice:

1. "cried constantly":
   suggests a state of permanent outrage
2. "mortal danger" :
   suggests extreme peril, life-threatening
3. "greedy":
   suggests they are over-eager for monetary gain
4. "only motive is profit":
   suggests single-minded quest for gain
5. "kept on roaring":
   suggests persistent expression of anger, aggression
6. "killing every wild thing in sight": use of hyperbole to express scale of destruction
7. "threatening the very soil":
   intensive, emphasising extent of menace
8. "overuse":
   suggests injury by excessive use
9. "continually … ululating":
   suggests constant loud lamentations

Sentence structure:

10. listing (lines 12-14):
    emphasises the range of alternatives which provoke protest
11. repetition of "or":
    suggests determination to find a source of complaint
12. Tripartite structure of "One faction has cried", "another has kept on roaring" and "still another … ululating" in three sections separated by semi-colons building to a climax of noisy dissent.

(b) *Possible answers*:

Word choice:

1. "proliferation":
   suggests excessive increase in numbers
2. "dedicated":
   suggests obsessiveness, misplaced devotion
3. "multifarious":
   suggests an inappropriate or confusing variety
4. "have become accustomed":
   suggests force of habit rather than genuine concern
5. "expending":
   suggests consumption to little purpose

6. "their time and energies":
   suggests an all-consuming obsession
7. "countless other aspects":
   suggests needless involvement in every area

Sentence structure:

8. list of features (lines 15-16):
   range of objections conveys excessive nature of protests
9. list of projects (lines 18-20):
   excessive concern about a wide range of aspects of nature

Tone:

10. "moorlands, uplands, lowlands":
    dismissive tone – as if "any old lands"
11. any of 1-9 above could be discussed in terms of a dismissive, scathing, contemptuous tone

3. (a) 1. "returned to the central position" refers to the aim of the action groups mentioned in lines 15-20 (no credit for the quotation unless the reference back is identified)

2. "worrying aspect" points forward to concerns the writer has (no credit for the quotation unless the reference forward is identified)

(b) 1. acceptable gloss on "identification … of the countryside in general and the landscape in particular with the past", eg that rural features are the only way of understanding our history

2. desire to preserve what is perceived as "our heritage"

3. difficulty in defining what is meant by the term "our heritage"

4. (a) *Any two of the following*:
   1. acceptable gloss on "our living link with our history" eg tangible, actual, real, visible connection with the past
   2. acceptable gloss on "the visible expression of our British roots" eg outward display, evidence of our heritage, identity
   3. failure to preserve the landscape will cause the connection to be lost

(b) *Any of the following*:
   1. who we are by race, our sense of belonging, does not stem from the physical setting in which we live
   2. there is no one connecting link between the countryside of today and the countryside of the past
   3. many diverse influences have joined to create a landscape which has suited the creators' own purposes

(c) *Possible answers*:
   1. "simply":
      pejorative, reductive view
   2. *"as it is now"*:
      use of italics stresses the conservationists' total rejection of change
   3. beginning sentence "Far from affirming history" emphasises mistaken approach

4. "affirming", "denies":
   juxtaposition of opposites reinforces the weakness of the conservationists' position
5. "actually": reinforces the contrast between affirmation and denial
6. "the continuous change without which history does not exist": final climactic assertion of writer's belief in direct opposition to the ideas of the conservationists

5. *Any three of the following*:
   1. it is impossible to define a point in time for the start of "tradition"
   2. conifers, which are unpopular nowadays, were significant in the past
   3. our more iconic species of trees (oak and elm) arrived much later
   4. animals (reindeer, rhinoceros, bison, hippopotamus, elephant) which have now vanished used to be abundant
   5. when man first appeared in Britain, the landscape was Arctic ice and tundra

6. (a) *Any two of the following*:
   1. hunting became more difficult …
   2. … as the grazing animals started to die out/became difficult to find …
   3. … because of increased afforestation

   (b) *Any of the following*:
   1. Stone Age man relied more on farming than on hunting
   2. he improved the efficiency of his farming tools
   3. he created space for grasslands for animals and/or crops
   4. crops were increasingly grown to serve man's needs

7. (a) the middle classes are not really worried about the countryside; what really concerns them is: gloss on "(the threat to) their own pleasure" **or** on "(the threat to) the value of their own property"

   (b) *Possible answers*:
   1. "heavy heart": deliberate exaggeration of the extent of his remorse
   2. "class traitor": inflated description suggesting his opinions constitute some terrible act/betrayal
   3. "middle-class, middle-aged property owner": writer deliberately casts himself as an archetype, clichéd representative of his class
   4. "smugly watched": suggests the writer is complacent, self-satisfied, gloating
   5. "soar in value":
      suggests a smug belief that his own success is both effortless and impressive
   6. "inordinately proud":
      suggests a pride which is hard to justify, excessive, out of all proportion
   7. "my view":
      suggests smug possessiveness
   8. "from an upstairs window":
      lampoons/undercuts the writer's pride in his view by suggesting the view is limited, inaccessible, awkward…

9. "motorway flyover in between":
   suggests something man-made, ugly, functional – ridiculing the writer's pride in his view
10. parenthesis (lines 7-8): apparently a throwaway qualification, but in reality used by the writer to highlight the overblown nature of his pride/undercut his argument
11. repetition of "(And) I" at the start of sentences: suggests self-absorbed, egotistical, pompous nature of middle classes
12. repetition of "I" followed by active verb: suggests an inflated belief in the importance of his actions/opinions
13. contrast: the ghastliness of his self-satisfied pride ("smugly watched", "soar in value") is heightened by the contrast with the desperation of the "young househunters" (In developing this point some candidates might choose to comment on the balance of "more and more"/"fewer and fewer".)

8. *Possible answers*:

Imagery:
1. "cherished credo":
   A "credo" is a religious belief. This suggests the reverence and/or depth of the middle classes" devotion to the countryside.
2. "forever sacrosanct":
   Something "sacrosanct" is sacred and untouchable. This implies an almost religious conviction that the countryside should remain unaltered, suggests the countryside is holy ground and changing it would be sacrilegious.
3. " 'Stalinist' decision": Stalin is considered to be an oppressive, ruthless dictator. This portrays the Government as dictatorial, evil, brutal, cruel, heartless …
4. "choked (by concrete)":
   Being "choked" involves strangulation, difficulty in breathing. This suggests the countryside is being destroyed, having the life squeezed out of it, unable to flourish, under attack.
5. "rapacious housebuilders":
   A "rapacious" act is a predatory one involving, for example, a bird of prey. This suggests the builders are aggressive, plundering, greedy, self-interested, voracious, gluttonous…
6. "devour whole landscapes":
   To "devour" something is to eat it up greedily. This suggests the builders are greedy, insatiable, all-consuming, indiscriminate…
7. "sprawling outward":
   To "sprawl" is to sit or lie in an awkward, ungainly way. This suggests the outward movement of the cities would be haphazard, unattractive, disorderly…
8. "will be swept away":
   "swept away" could refer to brushing or tidal movement. Either way, it suggests a rapid, extensive, conclusive end to the green belts.

Word choice:

9. "verdant hills and dales":
    idealised, Eden-like vision of the countryside as lush, fertile
10. "forever":
    intensifies belief in inviolable nature of the countryside
11. "impose":
    suggests compulsion, force, authoritarian government
12. "most hideous":
    superlatively repulsive, despicable, morally offensive
13. "threat":
    suggests pain, injury, a menacing, bullying enemy...
14. "our way of life":
    suggests a set of shared, traditional, important values
15. "since the Luftwaffe ... in 1940":
    (comparing the effect of more houses to the damage caused by German bombers) suggests they fear huge destruction, regard the builders as an evil, destructive, aggressive enemy
16. "cherished green belts":
    the countryside is loved and treasured
17. "14 great rings":
    majestic, impressive, powerful, important

Register:

18. candidates should be rewarded who make a sensible attempt to identify a register (inflated, over-the-top, exaggerated, mock-reverential, faux-outraged) and then – through appropriate reference and analysis – show how the writer's use of this register pokes fun at, attacks, exemplifies the views of the middle classes; any of the listed examples of imagery and word choice might be used to support such an answer

9. *Possible answers*:

Sentence structure:

1. the positioning of "Yet" at the start of the opening sentence sets up the rebuttal of the preceding argument
2. contrast/balance in opening sentence of "sweep away"/"look at" moves argument forward
3. structure of opening sentence places emphasis on principal clause at its conclusion
4. short, (apparently) concessionary 2nd sentence, introduced by "Yes", is immediately qualified/contradicted by 3rd sentence
5. positioning of "But" at start of 3rd sentence sets up qualification/ contradiction to 2nd sentence
6. repetition of "seem crowded" following "crowded" also underlines 3rd sentence's qualification/contradiction
7. short, punchy, declarative final two sentences drive home writer's point
8. positioning of "Just" at start of final sentence underlines (surprisingly small) statistic

9. candidates may comment on the writer's general sign-posting at the start of sentences: "Yet", "Yes", "But", "Just" to flag up the oppositional nature of his argument

Word choice:

10. "sweep away":
    suggests previous argument is "rubbish" and can be dealt with/dismissed very quickly
11. "apoplectic":
    suggests uncontrolled, irrational anger
12. "froth":
    suggests something insubstantial, trivial...
13. "self-interested":
    suggests middle classes only concerned with themselves, not the countryside
14. "posturing":
    suggests middle classes" concern is exaggerated, contrived, fake, affected ...
15. "look at the reality":
    suggests truth is clear and incontrovertible
16. "recedes dramatically":
    suggests rapid movement, significant diminution of threat
17. "overwhelmingly green":
    emphasises full extent of Britain's rural make-up
18. "classified":
    official nature of term reinforces accuracy, validity of statistic
19. use of personal pronouns ("you ... we ...us ...our"):
    clear attempt to make the reader share his point of view/involve the reader personally

10. (*a*) 1. gloss on "wasteland, largely devoid of landscape beauty": eg it is a wilderness, it is not attractive, it serves no purpose, it has no redeeming features and
    2. there is a desperate shortage of housing in London (for reasons of space and/or cost)

(*b*) *Possible answers*:

Word choice
1. "myth":
    suggests belief is untrue, fictitious, irrational, fanciful
2. "Well, lungs they might be":
    suggests reluctant, grudging, conditional acceptance of claim
3. "not at all": definitive, categorical negative

Sentence structure:

4. "Well, lungs they might be":
    inversion places emphasis on writer's doubt/scepticism
5. "But":
    position at start of sentence introduces idea of rebuttal
6. parenthesis (line 30):
    used to point out slyly that the middle classes benefit commercially as well as environmentally

10. (*b*) *continued*

7. progressive nature of final sentence: using semi-colons, the writer divides final sentence into three sections to stress the diminishing benefits of green belts **and/or** the diminishing benefits are also signposted structurally by the use of "chiefly", "and then" and "and not at all" at the start of each section

8. climax of final sentence:
   writer uses colon to introduce, direct attention to those who are not advantaged by green belts

Tone:

9. "Well, lungs they might be":
   dismissive, sceptical tone stresses his lack of belief

10. "nice houses", "leafy suburbs":
    use of clichés creates a rather mocking tone towards those enjoying a comfortable, carefree existence

11. "(not least … values sky-high)": ironic aside underlines writer's scepticism towards middle classes

Other language features:

12. any other acceptable suggestion supported by appropriate reference and explanation

11. First option (lines 33–37)

(*a*) *Possible answer*:
   green-belt protectionists believe they are protecting land which has been unchanged for centuries when in reality each generation has changed the land as required

(*b*) *Possible answers*:

Word choice:

1. "claim":
   suggests doubt/dubiety

2. "rampant advance":
   suggests insatiable demands; uses hyperbole to make their claims seem absurd, over the top, fanciful

3. "bulldozers" (used to symbolise builders):
   connotations of indiscriminate destruction, demolition; again suggests protectionists' claims are deliberately exaggerated, alarmist

4. "exactly what":
   suggests claims lack detail

5. "imagine":
   suggests green-belt protectionists are removed from reality, living in a dream world

6. "Primordial forest", "Boadicea", "the Romans":
   deliberate reference to very distant times/people stresses the unlikeliness of the green-belt campaigners' claims **or** implicit comparison of their claims to Boadicea's heroic life-or-death battle against a genuine aggressor highlights their pretension, self-importance, lack of perspective

7. "Hogwash":
   categorical condemnation – claims are worthless, false, ridiculous, "garbage"

8. "making and remaking":
   suggests change is ongoing, inevitable process

Sentence structure:

9. repetition of questions: hectoring, nagging, confrontational

10. single-word sentence: highlights his utter rejection of their claims

11. fluent, formal final sentence (in comparison to previous sentence): controlled, certain, assured, rational

Tone:

12. scornful/dubious – "claim"

13. satirical – "rampant advance"

14. dismissive/incredulous – "exactly what", "imagine"

15. humorous – "primordial", "Boadicea thrashed the Romans"

16. dismissive, contemptuous – deliberate informality of "Hogwash"

17. authoritative, certain – created by formality of final sentence (in contrast to the previous sentence)

11. Second option (lines 38–43)

(*a*) *Possible answers*:
   green-belt protectionists think the government is imposing change/being authoritarian but current planning laws are equally harsh/dictatorial **and/or** green-belt protectionists oppose the government's plans to build houses/change green belt planning but the existing planning laws have worked out poorly/been calamitous or are very protective of the countryside

(*b*) *Possible answers*:

Word choice:

1. "fond":
   suggests green-belt protectionists are self-indulgent, enjoy being critical

2. "deriding":
   suggests their arguments are cruel, contemptuous, destructive

3. "monstrous":
   deliberate exaggeration to make their claims seem excessive

4. "Soviet-style diktats":
   comparison to authoritarian state suggests green-belt protectionists' views are alarmist and excessive

5. "imagine":
   suggests their ideas are fanciful, unrealistic…

6. "disastrous":
   suggests horrific, life-threatening, widespread effects of existing laws

7. "impact":
   suggests powerful, negative, destructive force of existing laws

Sentence structure:
8. "Good grief":
   positioning at start of sentence establishes exasperated tone of diatribe to follow
9. "…and often disastrous,":
   adds additional layer of criticism
10. rhetorical question:
    stylistic device inviting reader to share the writer's beliefs
11. "not just … but":
    this construction allows the writer to expand his argument into other areas, build his argument to a climax
12. listing "on … on …on":
    repetitive structure suggests scale, variety of problems caused by current laws

Tone:
13. scornful – "fond"
14. satirical – "monstrous, Soviet-style diktats"
15. exasperated, frustrated, angry, incredulous – "Good grief", "what on earth do they imagine"
16. passionate, increasingly angry – "on employment … on economic growth?"

12. *Possible answers*

Ideas:
1. writer brings argument back to shortage of housing – a key issue introduced in the opening paragraph and referred to throughout the passage
2. writer focuses again on the selfishness, aggression, insularity, idealised views of the middle classes – themes discussed at various points throughout the passage.
3. writer looks at those affected ("young and poor") by the middle classes' campaigns and the problems they have (lack of housing, inability to advance themselves, long distances to travel to work) – attempting to damn the middle classes' opposition.

Style:
4. "And … on homelessness":
   link to or climax of argument from previous paragraph, returning argument to its primary concern
5. "homelessness":
   somewhat sensationalised term, a deliberate (and misleading?) attempt by the writer to evoke our sympathy
6. "Every time":
   wearisome inevitability of middle class campaigning
7. "bunch":
   suggests a gang or a loose grouping lacking authority or credibility; derogatory term continues criticism of middle classes
8. "fights off":
   criticism of middle classes' combative, aggressive stance
9. " 'intrusion' ":
   use of inverted commas reiterates misguided nature of middle class objections

10. "cherished landscape":
    satirical tone, once again poking fun at the middle classes" idealised, possessive vision of the countryside
11. "young and poor":
    attempt to tug at the readers' heartstrings and emphasise the cruelty of the middle classes' opposition
12. "reasonable proximity", "somewhere to live":
    the reasonable, understated goals of those seeking houses stand in contrast to the middle classes' unyielding, isolationist, unhelpful position
13. "pulling up drawbridge … castle": extended metaphor again suggests the insular/selfish, feudal, old-fashioned, elitist, uncaring, NIMBYist nature of the middle classes.

Question on both Passages

13. The mark for this question should reflect the overall quality of the response and may not be directly related to the length of the response or to the number of points/reference made. A succinct sophisticated response should be worth more than a series of fairly trivial points and obvious references.

For full marks there must be reference to both passages (although not necessarily a balanced treatment) and convincing evaluative comment.

Any of the points below would be valid comment:

Passage 1

Ideas
- surprise that there is such wide coverage of the countryside debate
- balance of ideas both past and present day
- awareness of the wide extent of claims put forward by conservationists
- strong feelings of those who feel the countryside is under threat
- writer's disapproval of action groups
- conservationists' view of our national identity is discredited
- concept of our national identity and the complexities involved
- history requires "continuous change"
- difficulties in establishing the "traditional British landscape"
- the landscape is determined by human influence not the environment

Style
- impersonal
- language used to highlight the strong feelings of conservationists: "so extensive …", "so fierce the passions …"
- repetition of "so"
- mocking tone
- word choice focusing on alleged dangers to the countryside: "mortal danger", "threatening", "killing", "overuse of machinery"
- tone of disapproval

13. *continued*

- word choice to discredit claims: "It might be thought", "widely assumed", "assumptions", "wildly overused term is seriously misleading"
- the short sentence to refute the claims: "This view is palpably nonsensical."
- imagery such as: "single thread", "bewildering array"
- balance of past/present
- impact of title/headline

Passage 2

Ideas

- the hypocrisy of the English middle classes regarding the countryside
- extreme nature of their view of the threat to the countryside
- the threat is much less serious than has been suggested
- some of the green belt around London should be used for housing
- the theory about green belts as "lungs" is a myth
- the flawed arguments of the "green-belt protectionists"
- green belts benefit property owners not those on inner city estates
- middle class homeowners react to any encroachment on their land and this makes it more difficult for the young and the poor to find suitable housing

Style

- personal involvement of the writer
- self-mocking tone regarding his own middle class position
- word choice to show extreme nature of the alleged threat to the countryside: "choked by concrete", "rapacious housebuilders"
- imagery in lines 11-19
- statistics in lines 20-24
- imagery in lines 25-32
- one-word sentence to dismiss claims made by conservationists: "Hogwash."
- conclusion: imagery of castle, drawbridge, …
- impact of title/headline

ENGLISH HIGHER CRITICAL ESSAY 2008

Please see the Critical Essay guidelines for the English Higher 2009 on page 22.

ENGLISH HIGHER
CLOSE READING 2009

1. (*a*) *Any two of the following*:

Acceptable gloss on/understanding of:

1. "absence of world war"	there is no world war/global conflict (to make travel difficult, dangerous)
2. "(unprecedented) prosperity"	people are well-off, wealthy (as never before)
3. "just as working people … generations"	travel has become democratic, available to all, no longer the sole preserve of the rich
4. "enjoy"	travel is fun, pleasurable, …
5. "other cultures … other climates"	travel allows people to experience different ways of life
6. "liberating possibilities"	travel broadens the mind, gives people greater insights into the world

(*b*) *Possible answers are*:

Sentence structure:

1. use of questions	first question is what politicians are asking the public to consider; second question shows the writer's incredulous response/immediate opposition **and/or** a case might be made that the repetition of the questions and/or the use of questions to open the passage indicates the combative, populist, anti-restriction stance of the writer
2. use of parenthesis in first paragraph ("the experience … climates")	to identify/exemplify the benefits/ freedoms of travel
3. use of list ("other cultures … climates")	to identify/exemplify the multiplicity of these benefits
4. repetition of "other"	to emphasise the multiplicity/variety of the experiences travel affords and/or to emphasise the very different nature of other countries
5. balanced structure of the "Just as … their reach" sentence	describing the many benefits of air travel in the first half of the sentence makes the negative thrust of its conclusion all the more forceful
6. use of "And" at start of second paragraph	unusual placement of conjunction is an eye-catching, forceful indication of the start of her personal opposition
7. use of parenthesis in second paragraph ("most of them comfortably off")	(rather sneering aside) to remind us that politicians are part of the rich elite who will still be able to travel/be unaffected by the restrictions
8. balanced structure/contrast of the "Maybe Tommy … social revelation" sentence	the writer concedes that there is a negative aspect to the democratisation of travel but shows the relative unimportance of this in the second half of the sentence via her sweeping affirmation of the large-scale benefits of travel

Continued

1. (*b*) *continued*

Word choice:	
9. "freedoms"	suggests that travel offers people independence, broadens their horizons, ...
10. "experience"	suggests something life-enhancing
11. "liberating (possibilities)"	suggests that travel allows people a freer, less constrained life-style
12. "enlightenment"	suggests travel can result in a fundamental increase/transformation in people's knowledge or happiness
13. "pleasure"	suggests enjoyment, gratification, ...
14. "(I reach for my) megaphone"	suggests strident, highly vocal, intense, I'm-standing-on-a-soapbox-and-you'd-better-listen opposition
15. "thousands (of people)"	suggests sheer number who have benefited from travel
16. "(would never have) ventured"	suggests limited nature of parents' experience as compared with current possibilities
17. "(social) revelation"	suggests life-changing benefit

2. *Four elements are required*:

1. "eco-lobby's anti-flying agenda" ...

2. ... refers back to the restrictive air travel proposals discussed in the opening two paragraphs;

3. "their strategy as a whole"/"can we just review"

4. ... leads into the discussion of the eco-lobby's proposed restrictions on travel as a whole/on energy use in general

3. (*a*) acceptable gloss on "creates intolerable pressure on the others" eg it puts (unbearable) stresses and strains on other forms of transport

(*b*) The nub of the answer lies in the information in lines 21-23: the congestion charge discouraged many commuters from driving into London and as a result London's train and tube services are now intolerably busy/putting prices up to reduce numbers.

4. (*a*) *Either or both of the following*:

1. mobility allows people to come together for a variety of beneficial reasons – for work, for pleasure and for people from different backgrounds to share knowledge/understand one another better (for full marks for this point alone, candidates will have to show reasonable understanding of "social/professional/cultural interactions")

2. many shared activities – which are only possible thanks to mobility – have made cities vital in the advancement of learning (for full marks for this point alone, candidates will have to show reasonable understanding of "centres of intellectual progress")

(*b*) Some candidates may identify a negative tone (angry, scathing, dismissive, sarcastic, caustic ...) or they may just assume the tone is one of "disapproval". Some candidates, however, may focus on the more positive, celebratory tone adopted by the writer in the second half of the paragraph which also conveys her disapproval of the anti-mobility "solution".

i. (b) *continued*

Possible answers are:

1. "and I am just waiting"	suggests writer's world-weary mistrust of politicians and the inevitability of their actions
2. "none/anywhere"	emphasising the extreme nature of the "solution"
3. "craven retreat"	suggests the "solution" would be a cowardly, unworthy, retrograde step
4. "Renaissance"	positive reference to a very enlightened, progressive, civilised period
5. "intellectual progress"	suggests society/civilisation moving forward in very considered, enlightened manner
6. parenthesis ("and I am … explicitly")	knowing aside to the readers about the bandwagon-joining propensities of politicians
7. "Stay at home and save the planet."	this parody of facile, instant sloganeering shows the writer's contempt for the quick-fix solutions of the eco-lobby
8. "social, professional and cultural"	accumulated list of benefits made possible by mobility
9. structure of the final sentence	the positioning (and the bluntness) of "But that" presages her explicit rejection of the "solution" **and/or** the dash (followed by "and") is used to introduce an additional point to the argument, effectively building the sentence to a resonant, powerful, pro-mobility climax

5. (*a*) Candidates need to show a basic understanding of "you'd still be making liberal use of the technology that has transformed domestic life": eg people would still use a lot of energy in their houses.

(*b*) *The following three key ideas for 1 mark each:*

1. (heating) has reduced/nearly eradicated certain (respiratory) diseases

2. (hot water/more effective cleaning) reduced/nearly eradicated disease-carrying pests/parasites/insects

3. (the car) has given people independence, broadened their horizons, made it easier for people to move about ("freedom") **or** (the car) has allowed people to be much more adaptable/less rigid, to have more choice in their lives ("flexibility")

(*c*) *Possible answers are*:

1. repetition of "Never mind …"	stresses her vehement, outraged opposition to so many of the restrictive measures (described previously) **and/or** the cumulative effect of having three sentences all starting with "Never mind" shows that she is opposed to the eco-lobby for a variety of reasons/on a variety of fronts
2. repetition in "the very young and the very old"	stresses that it is the most vulnerable members of society who would be put most at risk by such restrictions
3. parenthesis (dashes)	allows her to name two particularly frightening/dangerous diseases, thus underlining the vital importance of heating/extreme dangers in cutting down on heating
4. parenthesis (brackets)	allows her to show the horrific threat posed by these pests, "plague" being associated with widespread, uncontrollable death
5. parenthesis (commas)	the insertion of "Green Public Enemy Number One" allows the writer to slip in a satirical jab at (what she perceives as) the silly, over-the-top scaremongering of the eco-lobby

(d) It would bring back a very divided society, a society split into rich and poor, a society of haves and have-nots ("reconstructing a class divide") which would be very bad/disastrous/detrimental to the poor, the have-nots, the less fortunate, the disadvantaged.

6. (a) Any acceptable gloss, eg (a hypothesis that suggests) the end of the world, global disaster, human annihilation, …

(b) *The following two points for 1 mark each:*

1. it would not be possible to grow enough food to deal with the world's ever-increasing population

2. the only things which would prevent large-scale starvation would be comparably terrible events.

(c) *Any two of the following points*
Acceptable gloss on/understanding of:

1. "complexity of human behaviour"	people don't always conform to a pattern, behave as expected
2. "Population…responded to economic and social conditions"	the rate of population growth was determined by people's environment/ particular circumstances
3. "force of ingenuity", "inventiveness and innovation"	people were smarter/more resourceful than he imagined
4. "intensive farming … invention of pesticides …"	new farming methods and scientific advances dramatically increased the amount of food
5. "simple, fixed relation between numbers of people and amount of resource"	his basic assumptions were wrong: the ratio of people to food became more complex than he had imagined

7. *The following points could be made:*

1. "Warnings of catastrophe come and go"	suggests such warnings are transient, unimportant, not unusual; not worthy of the current over-reaction (a case might be made that the shortness of this sentence suggests a blunt, unequivocal dismissal on the writer's part)
2. "Whatever their validity"	suggests writer's scepticism
3. "we cannot and should not"	rhetorical repetition and cadence to emphasise, assertive, decisive opposition
4. "more restricted way of life"	suggests loss of freedom
5. "anyway"	dismissive tone, rejecting underlying concept of restrictions
6. "impracticable"	highlights fundamental flaws in the proposals
7. "grotesquely unfair"	suggests a monstrous, outlandish travesty of justice
8 "socially divisive"	suggests an attack on the very fabric of society
9. repetition of the "If" structure in the final two sentences	could be argued that this brings the passage to a climax: the penultimate sentence an emphatic summing-up of her objections, the final sentence an affirmation of her belief in human resourcefulness
10. repetition of "we" throughout paragraph	suggests writer is taking a stand for all of us; underlines her belief that this is something we can solve together as opposed to being dictated to by government
11. general use of pairs as a rhetorical device: "cannot and should not", "grotesquely unfair and socially divisive", "innovate and engineer"	candidates may find the repetitive use of this device gives the paragraph a persuasive certainty. On the other hand, they may find it somewhat repetitive, wearisome, contrived, mechanical, …

. (a) *Answers should show an understanding of*:

"how to square this urge… responsible citizen" eg the writer loves travelling/wants to fly but also wants to act sensibly/do the right thing/be free of guilt.

(b) *Possible answers are*:

Word choice:

1. "I", "my"	suggests the personal impact on his life
2. "desperate"	exaggerated sense of urgency, panic, distress
3. "loved"	suggests strong/deep personal attachment
4. "descended"	indicates the downward turn his life has taken
5. "near-permanent depression"	exaggerates dire consequences
6. "young (daughters)"	slightly manipulative reference to the young as innocent/vulnerable/representatives of future generations
7. "abstinence"	implies a sense of personal sacrifice

Sentence structure:

8. "Please someone…"	exaggerated sense of direct plea to anyone; (mock) melodramatic
9. rhetorical question "who doesn't ?"	to justify his argument by implying that his love of travel applies to everybody
10. parenthetical "and … young daughters"	sets himself up as caring family man; drives home extent of implications
11. use of questions	to highlight uncertainty/insecurity
12. repetition of "I", "my"	as point 1
Use of contrast:	
13. "at least"/"at best"	use of superlatives to highlight ultimate scenarios

Use of contrast:

13. "at least"/"at best"	use of superlatives to highlight ultimate scenarios

9. (a) There must be some indication that the candidate understands the term "irony". A "two-pronged" answer is required, in candidate's own words as far as possible.

The key point is that the conference is connected to "how damaging" flying is to the environment, yet delegates have "flown from around the world" to be there.

(b) *Possible answers are*:

Sentence structure:

1. repetition ("speaker after speaker")	to emphasise the sheer number of delegates of like mind, claiming victimisation of the industry …
2. use of colon	to introduce so-called justification for their case by singling out what they claim are even greater causes of pollution
3. use of questions in the final two sentences	designed to divert attention from their culpability

Word choice:

4. "bemoaned", "cried"	use of negative language to emphasise the self-pitying, whingeing nature of the delegates
5. "somehow"	suggests it has happened by chance/not based on logic

Continued

9. (*b*) *continued*

6. "…in perspective"	assumed rationality followed by obfuscation
7. "singled out", "chase after", "picking on"	presenting themselves as harassed victims
8. "efficiency savings"	delegates' euphemism to disguise effects on other industries
9. "gives so much to the world"	sanctimonious self-justification
10. "economically fragile"	supposed claims of being delicate, vulnerable, frail, …

Tone:

11. mocking, satirical, pejorative, belittling …	supported by sensible comment such as: - the use of reported speech (eg "Why … singled out?") to replicate sound of whingeing complaints - presentation of themselves as victimised underdogs - colloquial language ("small fry", "singled out", "chase after", "picking on") to present delegates as juvenile, shallow - "they cried … they said" creates sense of constant complaint … - or appropriate comment using any of points 1-10 above

(*c*) *Possible answers/comments are*:

1. "etched (over one another)".	just as etching involves cutting into a surface, using acid or a sharp implement, so the Earth will be permanently damaged by a crisscrossing indentation of flightpaths	2. "scarred"	just as a scar is a mark left by a wound, there will be permanent disfigurement to the Earth

10. *A gloss of the key points in lines 31-33 for 1 mark each, ie*:

1. to offset environmental cost ("the polluter must pay")

2. to reduce numbers of people flying ("to drive down demand")

11. *Possible answers are*:

1. "nice cuddly idea"	suggests something childish, spuriously comforting **and/or** use of colloquial language is incongruous when juxtaposed with scientific terminology beforehand
2. "on the surface"	suggests superficial thinking
3. references to Thailand and Honduras	selection of worthy activities/distant locations to convey relatively low-impact options
4. "handing out"	suggests a mere distribution exercise, an easy option, something rather patronising
5. "job done"	flippancy of short-term fix idea
6. "(simply) carry on flying"	clichéd, complacent attitude of those indifferent to looking for remedies
7. "regardless"	the last word in passage highlights irresponsibility

Question on both Passages

12. The mark for this question should reflect the overall quality of the response and may not be directly related to the length of response or to the number of points/references made. A succinct, sophisticated response should be worth more than a series of fairly trivial points and obvious references.

For full marks there must be a reference to both elements (ie ideas and style) and to both passages (although not necessarily a balanced treatment) and convincing evaluative comment.

Ideas – Passage 1:
- to save limited natural resources, threat of restrictions to freedom to travel
- opportunities to experience new places being denied
- advantages of air travel as "a social revelation"
- green taxes affect London road transport and rail fares, as well as air travel
- importance of travel to allow social, professional and cultural interaction
- proposed restrictions on scarce resources would also extend to our homes
- benefits of modern technology in preventing disease and providing freedom
- reconstruction of a new class divide would result from politicians' environmental restrictions
- possibility of mortal danger from global warming
- dire environmental warnings from the past have not been realised
- instead of unfair restrictions, we must devise a method of managing the predicted environmental crisis

Ideas – Passage 2
- conflict between desire to fly and duty to be a responsible citizen
- concern for the future and necessity of restricting flying
- map evidence of extent of current flightpaths
- presentation of stark choice between status quo or cutting back on air travel
- personal view that flying must become more expensive to reduce demand
- other remedies to offset the damage would merely mask the continuing problem caused by flying

Style – Passage 1
- use of questions to stimulate debate
- use of passionate language to convey strength of feeling about restricted travel
- introduction of exaggerated illustration
- reasoned debating style
- use of London congestion charge as an illustration
- use of a disapproving tone to ridicule proposed travel restrictions
- rhetorical, exhortatory repetition to convey view that removal of modern advances would be ludicrous
- introduction of historical example

Style – Passage 2
- use of conversational tone
- use of personal anecdote
- use of others' views to convey misconceptions about the damage caused by air travel
- introduction of emotionally charged comment to convey strength of feeling
- use of questions to convey the alternative sides of the debate

ENGLISH HIGHER CRITICAL ESSAY 2009

1. Judging against the Performance Criteria

Each essay should first be read to establish whether it achieves success in all the Performance Criteria below, including relevance and the standards for technical accuracy.

Understanding

As appropriate to task, the response demonstrates secure understanding of key elements, central concerns and significant details of the *text(s).

Analysis

The response explains accurately and in detail ways in which relevant aspects of structure/style/language contribute to meaning/effect/impact.

Evaluation

The response reveals clear engagement with the *text(s) or aspects of the text(s) and stated or implied evaluation of effectiveness, substantiated by detailed and relevant evidence from the *text(s).

Expression

Structure, style and language, including use of appropriate critical terminology, are deployed to communicate meaning clearly and develop a line of thought which is sustainedly relevant to purpose; spelling, grammar and punctuation are sufficiently accurate.

*The term "text" encompasses printed, audio or film/video text(s) which may be literary (fiction or non-fiction) or may relate to aspects of media or language.

2. Confirming Technical Accuracy

An essay which does not satisfy the requirement for "sufficient" technical accuracy cannot pass. If, however, technical accuracy is deemed "sufficient", then there are no penalties or deductions for such errors.

The definition of "sufficiently accurate" is the same as that given below for "consistently accurate", but with an allowance made for examination conditions, ie time pressure and no opportunity to redraft.

Consistently accurate (in line with Core Skills statement)

Few errors will be present. Paragraphs, sentences and punctuation are accurate and organised so that the writing can be clearly and readily understood. Spelling errors (particularly of high frequency words) are infrequent.

3. Assigning a Category and Mark

Each essay should then be assigned to the appropriate Category as outlined in the Broad Descriptors, supported by reference to the Detailed Descriptors.

(a) Broad Descriptors

Essays which **pass** (ie meet the minimum requirements of the Performance Criteria) should be assigned to one of four categories as follows:

Category	Mark(s)	Broad descriptor
I	25	Outstanding
II	21 **or** 23	Very sound
III	17 **or** 19	Comfortably achieves the Performance Criteria
IV	13 **or** 15	Just succeeds in achieving the Performance Criteria

Essays which **fail** to meet the minimum requirements of one or more than one Performance Criterion should be assigned to one of two categories as follows:

Category	Mark(s)	Broad descriptor
V	11 **or** 9	Fails to achieve one or more than one Performance Criterion and/or to achieve sufficient technical accuracy, or is simply too thin
VI*	7 **or** 5**	Serious shortcomings

In Categories II – VI, the choice of which mark to award should be determined by the level of certainty with which the response has been assigned to the Category.

* Essays in this Category will be extremely rare. It should be used only in cases of significant misunderstanding of a text, extreme thinness, or serious weaknesses in expression and/or technical accuracy.

** Marks below 5 could, in exceptional circumstances, be awarded – for example to a response which was of extreme brevity, perhaps just a few lines.

(b) Detailed descriptors

Category I (25 marks): A sophisticated response which, allowing for the pressures of examination conditions and the limited time available, is outstanding in nearly every respect. Knowledge and understanding of the text(s) are sound. The question is addressed fully and convincingly in such a way as to show insight into the text(s) as a whole, and selection of evidence to support the argument is extensive and skilful. The essay is effectively structured as a genuine response to the question. As appropriate to the task and the text(s), the candidate demonstrates a sophisticated awareness of the literary and/or linguistic techniques being exploited. There is a committed evaluative stance with respect to the text(s) and the task, although this is not necessarily explicit. Expression is controlled and fluent.

Dealing with longer texts, the response ranges effectively over the whole text where appropriate, selects effectively, and while focusing on the demands of the question, never loses sight of the text as a whole; dealing with shorter texts, the response uses a text which clearly allows the requirements of the question to be met fully, avoids "blanket coverage" and mechanistic, unfocused "analysis", and shows a pleasing understanding of the text as a whole.

Category II (21 or 23 marks): A very sound response which, allowing for the pressures of examination conditions and the limited time available, is secure in most respects. Knowledge and understanding of the text(s) are sound. The question is addressed fully in such a way as to show some insight into the text(s) as a whole, and selection of evidence to support the argument is extensive. The essay is soundly structured as a genuine response to the question. As appropriate to the task and the text(s), the candidate demonstrates a sound awareness of the literary and/or linguistic techniques being exploited. There is a clear evaluative stance with respect to the text(s) and the task, although this is not necessarily explicit. Expression is controlled.

Dealing with longer texts, the response ranges over the whole text where appropriate, selects sensibly, and while focusing on the demands of the question, never loses sight of the text as a whole; dealing with shorter texts, the response uses a text which clearly allows the requirements of the question to be met, avoids "blanket coverage" and mechanistic, unfocused "analysis", and shows a sound understanding of the text as a whole.

Category III (17 or 19 marks): A response which, allowing for the pressures of examination conditions and the limited time available, is secure in a number of respects. Knowledge and understanding of the text(s) are on the whole sound. The question is addressed adequately in such a way as to show understanding of the text as a whole, and selection of evidence to support the argument is appropriate to the task. The essay is structured in such a way as to meet the requirements of the question. As appropriate to the task and the text(s), the candidate shows an awareness of the literary and/or linguistic techniques being exploited. There is some evaluative stance with respect to the text(s) and the task, although this is not necessarily explicit. Expression is satisfactory.

Dealing with longer texts, the response makes some attempt to range over the whole text where appropriate, makes some selection of relevant evidence, and while focusing on the demands of the question, retains some sense of the text as a whole; dealing with shorter texts, the response uses a text which meets the requirements of the question, avoids excessive "blanket coverage" and mechanistic, unfocused "analysis", and shows an understanding of the text as a whole.

Category IV (13 or 15 marks): A response which, allowing for the pressures of examination conditions and the limited time available, just manages to meet the minimum standard to achieve the Performance Criteria. Knowledge and understanding of the text(s) are adequate. The question is addressed sufficiently in such a way as to show reasonable understanding of the text as a whole, and there is some evidence to support the argument. There is some evidence that the essay is structured in such a way as to meet the requirements of most of the question. As appropriate to the task and the text(s), the candidate shows some awareness of the literary and/or linguistic techniques being exploited. There is some evaluative stance with respect to the text(s) and the task, although this is not necessarily explicit. Expression is adequate.

Dealing with longer texts, the response retains some sense of the text as a whole; dealing with shorter texts, the response uses a text which meets the requirements of the question, avoids excessive use of mechanistic, unfocused "analysis", and shows some understanding of the text as a whole.

Category V (11 or 9 marks): A response will fall into this Category for a variety of reasons: it fails to achieve sufficient technical accuracy; or knowledge and understanding of the text are not deployed as a response relevant to the task; or any analysis attempted is undiscriminating and/or unfocused; or the answer is simply too thin.

Hey! I've done it

BrightRED
PUBLISHING

Published by Bright Red Publishing Ltd, 6 Stafford Street, Edinburgh, EH3 7AU
Tel: 0131 220 5804, Fax: 0131 220 6710, enquiries: sales@brightredpublishing.co.uk,
www.brightredpublishing.co.uk

Official SQA answers to 978-1-84948-057-4
2006-2009

Questions on Passage 2   *Marks*   *Code*

8. "The school was well-meaning—just misguided." (lines 16–17)
   (a) How do lines 1–15 demonstrate this?   2   U
   (b) Show how the writer's word choice in lines 7–15 makes clear the children's
       attitude to the school's ban.   2   A

9. Read lines 25–44.
   Identify what, according to the writer, is the "motivation" referred to in line 29,
   and show in your own words how it is illustrated in lines 36–44.   3   U

10. Show how the sentence structure in lines 45–51 highlights the writer's views
    about the obesity debate.   2   A

11. "A corrective to the scare tactics is needed." (lines 61–62)
    (a) Show how the language of lines 52–60 supports the connotation(s) of the
        expression "scare tactics".   2   A
    (b) Explain in your own words how lines 62–72 suggest a "corrective" to the scare
        tactics.   2   U

12. How does the writer's language in the final paragraph (lines 78–87) highlight her
    belief that action is required on this issue?   2   A

                                                                                               (15)

Questions on both Passages

13. Consider lines 1–45 of Passage 1 and lines 1–51 of Passage 2.

    In these lines each writer presents the opening stages of an argument about
    obesity.
    (a) Briefly state an important difference between the two **points of view** as set
        out in these lines.   1   U
    (b) By comparing the **style** of these lines, show which you find more effective in
        capturing your interest.   4   A/E

                                                                                               (5)

                                                                            Total (50)

[END OF QUESTION PAPER]

[BLANK PAGE]

X115/303

NATIONAL
QUALIFICATIONS
2006

FRIDAY, 12 MAY
10.50 AM – 12.20 PM

ENGLISH
HIGHER
Critical Essay

Answer **two** questions.

Each question must be taken from a different section.

Each question is worth 25 marks.

SCOTTISH
QUALIFICATIONS
AUTHORITY

Answer TWO questions from this paper. Each question must be chosen from a different Section (A–E). You are not allowed to choose two questions from the same Section.

In all Sections you may use Scottish texts.

Write the number of each question in the margin of your answer booklet.

You should spend about 45 minutes on each essay.

The following will be assessed:

- the relevance of your essays to the questions you have chosen, and the extent to which you sustain an appropriate line of thought

- your knowledge and understanding of key elements, central concerns and significant details of the chosen texts, supported by detailed and relevant evidence

- your understanding, as appropriate to the questions chosen, of how relevant aspects of structure/style/language contribute to the meaning/effect/impact of the chosen texts, supported by detailed and relevant evidence

- your evaluation, as appropriate to the questions chosen, of the effectiveness of the chosen texts, supported by detailed and relevant evidence

- the quality of your written expression and the technical accuracy of your writing.

SECTION A—DRAMA

Answers to questions on drama should address relevantly the central concern(s)/theme(s) of the text and be supported by reference to appropriate dramatic techniques such as: conflict, characterisation, key scene(s), dialogue, climax, exposition, dénouement, structure, plot, setting, aspects of staging (such as lighting, music, stage set, stage directions . . .), soliloquy, monologue . . .

1. Choose a play in which the dramatist's use of contrast between two characters is important to your understanding of one of them.

   Discuss how your understanding of this character is strengthened by the contrast.

2. Choose a play in which the conclusion leaves you with mixed emotions but clearly conveys the dramatist's message.

   Briefly explain how the mixed emotions are aroused by the conclusion and then discuss how you are given a clear understanding of the message of the play as a whole.

3. Choose a play which underlines how one person's flaw(s) can have a significant impact on other people as well as on himself or herself.

   Explain briefly the nature of the flaw(s) and then, in detail, assess how much the character and others are affected.

4. Choose a play in which an important theme is effectively highlighted by one specific scene or incident.

   Explain how the theme is explored in the play as a whole and then show in detail how the chosen scene or incident effectively highlights it.

SECTION B—PROSE

Prose Fiction

> *Answers to questions on prose fiction should address relevantly the central concern(s)/theme(s) of the text(s) and be supported by reference to appropriate techniques of prose fiction such as: characterisation, setting, key incident(s), narrative technique, symbolism, structure, climax, plot, atmosphere, dialogue, imagery . . .*

5. Choose a **novel** or **short story** in which a central character's failure to understand the reality of his or her situation is an important feature of the text.

    Explain how the writer makes you aware of this failure and show how it is important to your appreciation of the text as a whole.

6. Choose a **novel**, set in a time different from your own, with a theme relevant to the world today.

    Show how you are led to an appreciation of the theme's continuing relevance, despite its setting in time.

7. Choose a **novel** or **short story** which you feel has a particularly well-chosen title.

    Explain why you think the title helps you to appreciate the central idea(s) of the text.

8. Choose a **novel** in which a key incident involves rejection or disappointment or loss.

    Describe briefly the key incident and assess its significance to the text as a whole.

Prose Non-fiction

> *Answers to questions on prose non-fiction should address relevantly the central concern(s)/theme(s) of the text and be supported by reference to appropriate techniques of prose non-fiction such as: ideas, use of evidence, selection of detail, point of view, stance, setting, anecdote, narrative voice, style, language, structure, organisation of material . . .*

9. Choose an **essay** or **piece of journalism** which has made an impact on you because of its effective style.

    Discuss how the writer's style adds to the impact of the content.

10. Choose a **non-fiction text** which provides insight into a country or a personality or a lifestyle.

    Describe briefly the country or personality or lifestyle and discuss the means by which the writer leads you to this insight.

11. Choose a **non-fiction text** which explores a significant aspect of political or cultural life.

    Show how the writer's presentation enhances your understanding of the chosen aspect of political or cultural life.

[Turn over

SECTION C—POETRY

> *Answers to questions on poetry should address relevantly the central concern(s)/theme(s) of the text(s) and be supported by reference to appropriate poetic techniques such as: imagery, verse form, structure, mood, tone, sound, rhythm, rhyme, characterisation, contrast, setting, symbolism, word choice . . .*

12. Choose a poem in which there is a noticeable change of mood at one or more than one point in the poem.

    Show how the poet conveys the change(s) of mood and discuss the importance of the change(s) to the central idea of the poem.

13. Choose a poem which deals with a childhood experience.

    Discuss to what extent the poet's description of the experience leads you to a clear understanding of the poem's theme.

14. Choose **two** poems by the same poet which you consider similar in theme and style.

    By referring to theme and style in both poems, discuss which poem you prefer.

15. Choose a poem which explores one of the following subjects: bravery, compassion, tenderness.

    Show how the poet's exploration of the subject appeals to you emotionally and/or intellectually.

SECTION D—FILM AND TV DRAMA

> *Answers to questions on film and TV drama should address relevantly the central concern(s)/theme(s) of the text(s) and be supported by reference to appropriate techniques of film and TV drama such as: key sequence(s), characterisation, conflict, structure, plot, dialogue, editing/montage, sound/soundtrack, aspects of mise-en-scène (such as lighting, colour, use of camera, costume, props . . .), mood, setting, casting, exploitation of genre . . .*

16. Choose a **film** or ***TV drama** the success of which is built on a central figure carefully constructed to appeal to a particular audience.

    Show how the film or programme makers construct this figure and explain why he/she/it appeals to that particular audience.

17. Choose a **film** or ***TV drama** in which a power struggle shapes the lives of key characters and/or groups.

    Discuss how effectively the film or programme makers establish the power struggle and go on to explain how it shapes the lives of the key characters and/or groups.

18. Choose a **film** in which the film makers have presented an epic story to critical and/or box office acclaim.

    Show how the film makers convey key epic elements and explain why you think the film has received such acclaim.

19. Choose a **film** or ***TV drama** which is based on a novel and successfully captures such elements of the book as setting, character, mood and theme.

    Show how the film or programme makers successfully capture any two elements of the novel.

*"TV drama" includes a single play, a series or a serial.

[Turn over

SECTION E—LANGUAGE

> *Answers to questions on language should address relevantly the central concern(s) of the language research/study and be supported by reference to appropriate language concepts such as: register, jargon, tone, vocabulary, word choice, technical terminology, presentation, illustration, accent, grammar, idiom, slang, dialect, structure, vocabulary, point of view, orthography, abbreviation . . .*

20. Consider the use of language to influence public opinion.

    Identify some of the ways in which language is used to influence the public's view on an issue of public interest. Evaluate the success of at least two of these ways.

21. Consider some of the differences between spoken language used in informal contexts and spoken language used in formal contexts.

    Identify some of the areas of difference and show to what extent the different forms are effective for the contexts in which they are used.

22. Consider the language—spoken or written—which is typically used by a group of people with a common leisure or vocational interest.

    To what extent is the specialist language effective in:

    • describing the details and procedures connected with the group's common interest and/or

    • reinforcing the interaction within the group?

23. Consider any one electronic means of communication introduced over the last forty years or so.

    To what extent has your chosen means of communication developed its own form of language? By examining aspects of this language discuss what you feel are its advantages and/or disadvantages.

[END OF QUESTION PAPER]

HIGHER

2007

[BLANK PAGE]

X115/301

NATIONAL
QUALIFICATIONS
2007

FRIDAY, 11 MAY
9.00 AM – 10.30 AM

ENGLISH
HIGHER
Close Reading—Text

There are TWO passages and questions.

Read the passages carefully and then answer all the questions, which are printed in a separate booklet.

You should read the passages to:

understand what the writers are saying about the proposal to put online the contents of some major libraries (**Understanding—U**);

analyse their choices of language, imagery and structures to recognise how they convey their points of view and contribute to the impact of the passage (**Analysis—A**);

evaluate how effectively they have achieved their purpose (**Evaluation—E**).

SCOTTISH
QUALIFICATIONS
AUTHORITY

PASSAGE 1

In the first passage George Kerevan, writing in The Scotsman *newspaper in December 2003, responds to the prospect of an "online library".*

DESPITE GOOGLE, WE STILL NEED GOOD LIBRARIES

The internet search engine Google, with whom I spend more time than with my loved ones, is planning to put the contents of the world's greatest university libraries online, including the Bodleian in Oxford and those of Harvard and Stanford in America. Part of me is ecstatic at the thought of all that information at my
5 fingertips; another part of me is nostalgic, because I think physical libraries, book-lined and cathedral-quiet, are a cherished part of civilisation we lose at our cultural peril.

My love affair with libraries started early, in the Drumchapel housing scheme in the Fifties. For the 60,000 exiles packed off from slum housing to the city's outer
10 fringe, Glasgow Council neglected the shops and amenities but somehow remembered to put in a public library—actually, a wooden shed. That library was split into two—an adult section and a children's section. This was an early taste of forbidden fruit. Much useful human reproductive knowledge was gained from certain books examined surreptitiously in the adult biology section.

15 At university, I discovered the wonder of the library as a physical space. Glasgow University has a skyscraper library, built around a vast atrium stretching up through the various floors. Each floor was devoted to a different subject classification. Working away on the economics floor, I could see other students above or below—chatting, flirting, doodling, panicking—all cocooned in their own separate
20 worlds of knowledge. Intrigued, I soon took to exploring what was on these other planets: science, architecture, even a whole floor of novels. The unique aspect of a physical library is that you can discover knowledge by accident. There are things you know you don't know, but there are also things you never imagined you did not know.

25 There is a stock response to my love affair with libraries: that I am being too nostalgic. That the multi-tasking, MTV generation can access information from a computer, get cheap books from the supermarket and still chatter to each other at a thousand decibels. Who needs old-fashioned library buildings? And why should councils subsidise what Google will provide for free?

30 There is some proof for this line of argument. The number of people in Scotland using their local public library falls every year, with just under a quarter of Scots now borrowing books (admittedly, that was 34 million books). As a result, local authorities have reduced their funding for new books by 30 per cent. Of course, fewer new books mean fewer library users, so guaranteeing the downward spiral.

35 It may well be that public demand and technical change mean we no longer need the dense neighbourhood network of local libraries of yore. But our culture, local and universal, does demand strategically situated libraries where one can find the material that is too expensive for the ordinary person to buy, or too complex to find online. Such facilities are worth funding publicly because the return in informed
40 citizenship and civic pride is far in excess of the money spent.

Libraries also have that undervalued resource—the trained librarian. The ultimate Achilles' heel of the internet is that it presents every page of information as being

equally valid, which is of course nonsense. The internet is cluttered with false information, or just plain junk. The library, with its collection honed and developed
45 by experts, is a guarantee of the quality and veracity of the information contained therein, something that Google can never provide.

Libraries have another function still, which the internet cannot fulfil. Libraries, like museums, are custodians of knowledge—and should be funded as such. It has become the fashion in recent decades to turn our great national libraries and
50 museums into entertainment centres, with audio-visuals, interactive displays and gimmicks. While I have some enthusiasm for popularising esoteric knowledge, it cannot always be reduced to the level of a child's view of the universe. We have a duty to future generations to invest in the custodians of our culture, in particular its literature and manuscripts.

55 Of course, I can't wait for Google to get online with the Bodleian Library's one million books. Yet here's one other thing I learned from a physical library space: the daunting scale of human knowledge and our inability to truly comprehend even a fraction of it. On arriving at Glasgow University library, I did a quick calculation of how many economics books there were on the shelves and realised that I could
60 not read them all. Ever. From which realisation comes the beginning of wisdom—and that is very different from merely imbibing information.

PASSAGE 2

In the second passage Ben Macintyre, writing in The Times *newspaper, also in December 2003, responds to the same news, and considers the future of the "traditional library".*

PARADISE IS PAPER, PARCHMENT AND DUST

I have a halcyon library memory. I am sitting under a cherry tree in the tiny central courtyard of the Cambridge University Library, a book in one hand and an almond slice in the other. On the grass beside me is an incredibly pretty girl. We are surrounded by eight million books. Behind the walls on every side of the
5 courtyard, the books stretch away in compact ranks hundreds of yards deep, the shelves extending at the rate of two miles a year. There are books beneath us in the subterranean stacks, and they reach into the sky; we are entombed in words, an unimaginable volume of collected knowledge in cold storage, quiet and vast and waiting.

10 Perhaps that was the moment I fell in love with libraries.

Or perhaps it was earlier, growing up in Scotland, when the mobile library would lurch up the road with stocks of Enid Blyton for the kids and supplies of bodice-rippers on the top shelf with saucy covers, to be giggled over when the driver-librarian was having his cup of tea.

15 Or perhaps the moment came earlier yet, when my father took me deep into the Bodleian in Oxford and I inhaled, for the first time, that intoxicating mixture of paper, parchment and dust.

I have spent a substantial portion of my life since in libraries, and I still enter them with a mixture of excitement and awe. I am not alone in this. Veneration for
20 libraries is as old as writing itself, for a library is more to our culture than a

collection of books: it is a temple, a symbol of power, the hushed core of civilisation, the citadel of memory, with its own mystique, social and sensual as well as intellectual.

But now a revolution, widely compared to the invention of printing itself, is taking
25 place among the book shelves, and the library will never be the same again. This week Google announced plans to digitise fifteen million books from five great libraries, including the Bodleian.

Some fear that this total library, vast and invisible, could finally destroy traditional libraries, which will become mere warehouses for the physical objects, empty of
30 people and life. However, the advantages of a single scholarly online catalogue are incalculable and rather than destroying libraries, the internet will protect the written word as never before, and render knowledge genuinely democratic. Fanatics always attack the libraries first, dictators seek to control the literature, elites hoard the knowledge that is power. Shi Huangdi, the Chinese emperor of the 3rd century BC,
35 ordered that all literature, history and philosophy written before the founding of his dynasty should be destroyed. More books were burnt in the 20th century than any other—in Nazi Germany, Bosnia and Afghanistan. With the online library, the books will finally be safe, and the bibliophobes will have been beaten, for ever.

But will we bother to browse the shelves when we can merely summon up any book
40 in the world with the push of a button? Are the days of the library as a social organism over? Almost certainly not, for reasons psychological and, ultimately, spiritual. Locating a book online is one thing, reading it is quite another, for there is no aesthetic substitute for the physical object; the computer revolution rolls on inexorably, but the world is reading more paper books than ever.

45 And the traditional library will also survive, because a library is central to our understanding of what it is to be human. Libraries are not just for reading in, but for sociable thinking, exploring and exchanging ideas. They were never silent. Technology will not change that, for even in the starchiest heyday of Victorian self-improvement, libraries were intended to be meeting places of the mind, recreational
50 as well as educational. The Openshaw branch of the Manchester public library was built complete with a billiard room. Of course just as bookshops have become trendy, offering brain food and cappuccinos, so libraries, under financial and cultural pressure, will have to evolve by more actively welcoming people in to wander and explore . . . and fall in love.

55 Bookish types have always feared change and technology, but the book, and the library, have adapted and endured, retaining their essential magic. Even Hollywood understood. In the 1957 film *Desk Set*, Katherine Hepburn plays a librarian-researcher whose job is threatened by a computer expert (Spencer Tracy) introducing new technology. In the end, the computer turns out to be an asset, not a
60 danger, Tracy and Hepburn end up smooching, and everyone reads happily ever after.

The marriage of Google and the Bodleian will surely be the same.

[END OF TEXT]

X115/302

NATIONAL QUALIFICATIONS 2007	FRIDAY, 11 MAY 9.00 AM – 10.30 AM	**ENGLISH** **HIGHER** Close Reading–Questions

Answer all questions. **Use your own words whenever possible and particularly when you are instructed to do so.**

50 marks are allocated to this paper.

A code letter (U, A, E) is used alongside each question to give some indication of the skills being assessed. The number of marks attached to each question will give some indication of the length of answer required.

SCOTTISH
QUALIFICATIONS
AUTHORITY

Questions on Passage 1

Marks　Code

1. Read lines 1–7.

   (a) What two contrasting emotions does the writer have about the plan to put the great university libraries online? Use your own words in your answer.　2　U

   (b) How does the writer's word choice in these lines help to convey his view of the importance of "physical libraries" (line 5)? Refer to **two** examples in your answer.　2　A

2. In your opinion, does the writer think Glasgow Council gave the library in Drumchapel a high priority? Justify your answer by close reference to lines 8–14.　2　U/E

3. Show how the writer uses imagery **and** word choice in lines 15–24 to convey the "wonder of the library as a physical space".　4　A

4. Read lines 25–34.

   (a) Show how the writer's language in lines 25–29 conveys his attitude to the "MTV generation". You should refer in your answer to such features as sentence structure, word choice, tone . . .　3　A

   (b) Explain the "downward spiral" (line 34) to which the writer refers.　1　U

5. (a) In your own words as far as possible, give **four** reasons the writer presents in lines 35–46 in favour of maintaining traditional public libraries.　4　U

   (b) Show how the writer's word choice in lines 41–46 emphasises the contrast between his attitude to libraries and his attitude to the internet.　2　A

6. Read lines 47–54.

   (a) Twice in this paragraph the writer refers to libraries as "custodians". What does this word mean?　1　U

   (b) Show how the language of lines 47–54 suggests that the writer has some reservations about the entertainment aspect of present day libraries and museums.　2　A

7. How effective do you find the ideas and/or language of the final paragraph (lines 55–61) as a conclusion to the passage as a whole?　3　E

(26)

Questions on Passage 2   *Marks   Code*

8. Read lines 1–17.

   (a) Briefly describe the mood created in lines 1–3 ("I have . . . girl.").   1   U

   (b) Show how the writer's use of language in lines 3–9 ("We are . . . waiting.") conveys a sense of awe.   3   A

   (c) How effective do you find the repetition of "perhaps" (lines 10–17) in conveying the writer's recollections about libraries?   2   A/E

9. By referring to **one** example, show how the writer's imagery in lines 18–23 conveys the importance of libraries.   2   A

10. Read lines 24–38.

    In your own words as far as possible, explain:

    (a) what, according to the writer, the potential disadvantage of the online library is;   1   U

    (b) what, according to the writer, the advantages of the online library are.   3   U

11. Read lines 39–54.

    (a) Explain what the writer means by "there is no aesthetic substitute for the physical object" (lines 42–43).   2   U

    (b) Using your own words as far as possible, explain why the writer believes libraries will "survive" (line 45).   2   U

12. How effectively does the writer use the reference to the film *Desk Set* to conclude the passage in a pleasing way? Refer in your answer to the ideas and language of lines 55–62.   3   E

                                                                              (19)

Question on both Passages

13. Which of the two writers do you think presents the more persuasive argument in favour of public libraries?

    Justify your choice by referring to the **ideas and style** of **both** passages.   5   E

                                                                               (5)

                                                                    Total **(50)**

[END OF QUESTION PAPER]

[BLANK PAGE]

X115/303

NATIONAL
QUALIFICATIONS
2007

FRIDAY, 11 MAY
10.50 AM – 12.20 PM

ENGLISH
HIGHER
Critical Essay

Answer **two** questions.

Each question must be taken from a different section.

Each question is worth 25 marks.

SCOTTISH
QUALIFICATIONS
AUTHORITY

Answer **TWO** questions from this paper. Each question must be chosen from a different Section (A–E). You are not allowed to choose two questions from the same Section.

In all Sections you may use Scottish texts.

Write the number of each question in the margin of your answer booklet and begin each essay on a fresh page.

You should spend about 45 minutes on each essay.

The following will be assessed:

- the relevance of your essays to the questions you have chosen, and the extent to which you sustain an appropriate line of thought

- your knowledge and understanding of key elements, central concerns and significant details of the chosen texts, supported by detailed and relevant evidence

- your understanding, as appropriate to the questions chosen, of how relevant aspects of structure/style/language contribute to the meaning/effect/impact of the chosen texts, supported by detailed and relevant evidence

- your evaluation, as appropriate to the questions chosen, of the effectiveness of the chosen texts, supported by detailed and relevant evidence

- the quality of your written expression and the technical accuracy of your writing.

SECTION A—DRAMA

Answers to questions on drama should address relevantly the central concern(s)/theme(s) of the text and be supported by reference to appropriate dramatic techniques such as: conflict, characterisation, key scene(s), dialogue, climax, exposition, dénouement, structure, plot, setting, aspects of staging (such as lighting, music, stage set, stage directions . . .), soliloquy, monologue . . .

1. Choose a play which has a theme of revenge or betrayal or sacrifice.

   Show how the dramatist explores your chosen theme and discuss how this treatment enhances your appreciation of the play as a whole.

2. Choose from a play an important scene which you found particularly entertaining or particularly shocking.

   Explain briefly why the scene is important to the play as a whole and discuss in detail how the dramatist makes the scene so entertaining or shocking.

3. Choose a play in which a character makes a crucial error.

   Explain what the error is and discuss to what extent it is important to your understanding of the character's situation in the play as a whole.

4. Choose a play in which the relationship between a male and a female character changes significantly.

   Show how the relationship between the two characters changes and discuss to what extent this illuminates a central idea of the play.

SECTION B—PROSE

Prose Fiction

> *Answers to questions on prose fiction should address relevantly the central concern(s)/theme(s) of the text(s) and be supported by reference to appropriate techniques of prose fiction such as: characterisation, setting, key incident(s), narrative technique, symbolism, structure, climax, plot, atmosphere, dialogue, imagery . . .*

5. Choose a **novel** in which a character reaches a crisis point.

    Explain briefly how this point is reached and go on to discuss how the character's response to the situation extends your understanding of him/her.

6. Choose **two short stories** in which aspects of style contribute significantly to the exploration of theme.

    Compare the ways in which stylistic features are used to create and maintain your interest in the central ideas of the texts.

7. Choose a **novel** with an ending which you found unexpected.

    Explain briefly in what way the ending is unexpected and go on to discuss to what extent it is a satisfactory conclusion to the novel.

8. Choose a **novel** or **short story** in which one of the main characters is not in harmony with her/his society.

    Describe the character's situation and go on to discuss how it adds to your understanding of a central concern of the text.

Prose Non-fiction

> *Answers to questions on prose non-fiction should address relevantly the central concern(s)/theme(s) of the text and be supported by reference to appropriate techniques of prose non-fiction such as: ideas, use of evidence, selection of detail, point of view, stance, setting, anecdote, narrative voice, style, language, structure, organisation of material . . .*

9. Choose a work of **non-fiction** which deals with **travel** or **exploration** or **discovery**.

    Discuss to what extent the presentation of the text reveals as much about the writer's personality and/or views as it does about the subject matter.

10. Choose a **biography** or **autobiography** in which the life of the subject is presented in an effective and engaging way.

    Show how the writer uses techniques of non-fiction to achieve this.

11. Choose an **essay** or **piece of journalism** which appeals to you because it is both informative and passionate.

    Explain what you learned about the topic and discuss how the writer's presentation conveys his/her passion.

[Turn over

SECTION C—POETRY

> *Answers to questions on poetry should address relevantly the central concern(s)/theme(s) of the text(s) and be supported by reference to appropriate poetic techniques such as: imagery, verse form, structure, mood, tone, sound, rhythm, rhyme, characterisation, contrast, setting, symbolism, word choice . . .*

12. Choose a poem in which there is a sinister atmosphere or person or place.

Show how the poet evokes this sinister quality and discuss how it adds to your appreciation of the poem.

13. Choose **two** poems on the same theme which impress you for different reasons.

Compare the treatment of the theme in the two poems and discuss to what extent you find one more impressive than the other.

14. Choose a poem in which there is effective use of one or more of the following: verse form, rhythm, rhyme, repetition, sound.

Show how the poet effectively uses the feature(s) to enhance your appreciation of the poem as a whole.

15. Choose a poem involving a journey which is both literal and metaphorical.

Discuss how effectively the poet describes the journey and makes you aware of its deeper significance.

SECTION D—FILM AND TV DRAMA

> *Answers to questions on film and TV drama should address relevantly the central concern(s)/theme(s) of the text(s) and be supported by reference to appropriate techniques of film and TV drama such as: key sequence(s), characterisation, conflict, structure, plot, dialogue, editing/montage, sound/soundtrack, aspects of mise-en-scène (such as lighting, colour, use of camera, costume, props . . .), mood, setting, casting, exploitation of genre . . .*

16. Choose a **film** or **TV drama*** the success of which is built on a rivalry or friendship between two characters.

    Show how the film or programme makers construct the characters and discuss how the rivalry or friendship contributes to the success of the text.

17. Choose a **film** in which music makes a significant contribution to the impact of the film as a whole.

    Show how the film makers make use of music, and go on to explain how its contribution is so important relative to other elements of the text.

18. Choose a **film** or **TV version** of a stage play or of a novel.

    By referring to key elements of the film or TV version, explain to what extent you think the film or programme makers were successful in transferring the play or novel to the screen.

19. Choose a **film** or **TV drama*** in which setting and atmosphere contribute more than plot to your appreciation of the text.

    Justify your opinion by referring to these elements of the text.

*"TV drama" includes a single play, a series or a serial.

[Turn over

SECTION E—LANGUAGE

> *Answers to questions on language should address relevantly the central concern(s) of the language research/study and be supported by reference to appropriate language concepts such as: register, jargon, tone, vocabulary, word choice, technical terminology, presentation, illustration, accent, grammar, idiom, slang, dialect, structure, point of view, orthography, abbreviation . . .*

20. Consider the spoken or written language of a particular geographical area. (This could be, for example, a village, a city, or a larger area of the UK.)

Identify what is distinctive about the language and evaluate the effects of these distinctive usages on the communication of the people of that area.

21. Consider the language of popular entertainment in the 21st century—in TV, radio, music, magazines, for example.

Describe how the idioms and vocabulary popularised by the entertainment industry influence the everyday speech of the younger generation. Discuss to what extent these usages enrich everyday communication.

22. Consider the language of persuasion employed in a commercial, political, social or personal situation.

Identify and discuss the effectiveness of several ways in which the language you have chosen attempts to be persuasive.

23. Consider the language typical of any particular vocational or interest group with which you are familiar.

To what extent are the specialist terms and idioms typical of this group a barrier to the ability of the general public to understand the communication? How necessary do you think these terms and idioms are for effective communication within the group?

[END OF QUESTION PAPER]

HIGHER

2008

[BLANK PAGE]

X115/301

NATIONAL QUALIFICATIONS 2008	THURSDAY, 15 MAY 9.00 AM – 10.30 AM	**ENGLISH** HIGHER Close Reading—Text

There are TWO passages and questions.

Read the passages carefully and then answer all the questions, which are printed in a separate booklet.

You should read the passages to:

understand what the writers are saying about the countryside and those who campaign to protect it (**Understanding—U**);

analyse their choices of language, imagery and structures to recognise how they convey their points of view and contribute to the impact of the passage (**Analysis—A**);

evaluate how effectively they have achieved their purpose (**Evaluation—E**).

PASSAGE 1

In this extract from his book "Shades of Green", David Sinclair looks at attitudes to the countryside and discusses to what extent it is part of "our heritage".

RURAL MANIA

The "countryside debate" has rarely been out of the news in Britain in recent years. Reading the newspapers, watching television, listening to the radio, entering a bookshop, one could be forgiven for thinking that we still live in small peasant communities dependent upon the minutest shift in agricultural policy. Sometimes it
5 has seemed almost as if we were still in the early nineteenth century when we relied on the countryside to survive, so extensive have been the debates, so fierce the passions aroused.

One faction has cried constantly that the countryside is in mortal danger from greedy developers whose only motive is profit; another has kept on roaring that
10 farmers are killing every wild thing in sight and threatening the very soil on which we stand through overuse of machinery and chemicals; still another has been continually heard ululating over a decline in the bird population, or the loss of hedgerows, or the disappearance of marshland, or the appearance of coniferous forest.

15 Then there is the proliferation of action groups dedicated to stopping construction of roads, airports, railway lines, factories, shopping centres and houses in rural areas, while multifarious organisations have become accustomed to expending their time and energies in monitoring and reporting on the state of grassland, water, trees, moorlands, uplands, lowlands, birds' eggs, wildflowers, badgers, historical sites and
20 countless other aspects of the landscape and its inhabitants.

It might be thought—indeed, it is widely assumed—that it must be good for the countryside to be returned to the central position it enjoyed in British life long ago. Yet there is a particularly worrying aspect of the new rural mania that suggests it might finally do the countryside more harm than good.

25 This is the identification, in the current clamour, of the countryside in general and the landscape in particular with the past—the insistence on the part of those who claim to have the best intentions of ruralism at heart that their aim is to protect what they glibly refer to as "our heritage". This wildly over-used term is seriously misleading, not least because nobody appears ever to have asked what it means.

30 The assumption is that the landscape is our living link with our history, the visible expression of our British roots, and that if we allow it to change ("to be destroyed", the conservationists would say), the link is broken forever. This view is palpably nonsensical. Our national identity is not defined by the landscape against which we carry on our lives. There is, in fact, no single thread that can be identified as our
35 rural heritage or tradition. Rather there is a bewildering array of different influences that have combined haphazardly through the centuries as successive invaders and immigrants and, later, successive generations, have reconstructed the landscape according to their own needs and ideas. What the conservationists seek to preserve is simply the landscape *as it is now*, in its incarnation of the early twenty-
40 first century. Far from affirming history, this approach actually denies it, for it would remove the continuous change without which history does not exist.

Where, for example, does the "traditional" landscape begin and end? If we take the period when the British Isles were born, nearly 8,000 years ago, we discover that the

conifers so hated by the conservationists today were one of the most important
45 features of the scenery; the "English" oak and the much-loved elm were later
immigrants from the warmer south. As for fauna, our "traditional" species included
reindeer, rhinoceros, bison, hippopotamus and elephant. But where are they now?

Perhaps we should do better in the search for our heritage to consider what the
countryside looked like when man first appeared in what we think of as Britain.
50 That would take us back 35,000 years, to the emergence of our ancestor *Homo
sapiens*, who found himself in an Arctic landscape of ice and tundra. The remnants
of that traditional scene can be found only in the highest mountains of Scotland; the
rest of Britain has changed beyond recognition.

Obviously, then, we must look at more recent times if we are to discover identifiable
55 traditional elements in the landscape we now see about us. Yet if we do that, further
difficulties emerge. The retreat of the last glaciation almost 11,000 years ago was
accompanied by a relatively rapid warming of the climate, which gradually
converted the open Arctic tundra into dense forest. This presented a serious
challenge to Stone Age man, who began to find that the grazing animals, which he
60 hunted for food, were disappearing as their habitat retreated before the encroaching
trees. In order to survive, he was forced to turn increasingly from hunting to
farming, with the dramatic effects on flora and fauna that remain familiar to us
today. As the quality of prehistoric tools improved, some stretches of forest were
felled to provide grazing for domesticated animals, while grasses and cereals were
65 deliberately encouraged because of their usefulness to man. Even the shape of the
countryside was changed as mining began to cut into hillsides, and in some places
soil deterioration set in as the growing populations demanded perhaps the earliest
form of intensive farming. In other words, the chief influence on the landscape of
these islands was not nature but mankind.

PASSAGE 2

*In the second passage, the journalist Richard Morrison responds to criticism of a Government
plan to allow a million new houses to be built in southeast England.*

PULLING UP THE DRAWBRIDGE

The English middle classes are rarely more hypocritical than when waxing
indignant about "the threat to the countryside". What anguishes them usually
turns out to be the threat to their own pleasure or to the value of their property.
And I write those sentences with the heavy heart of a class traitor, for I am a
5 middle-class, middle-aged property owner who has smugly watched his own house
soar in value as more and more young househunters desperately chase fewer and
fewer properties. I am inordinately proud of my view across the green belt (from
an upstairs window admittedly, because of the motorway flyover in between). And
I intend to spend the weekend rambling across the rural England I have loved since
10 boyhood.

The most cherished credo of the English middle classes is that the verdant hills
and dales of the Home Counties should remain forever sacrosanct, and that the
Government's "Stalinist" decision to impose a million extra houses on southeast
England is the most hideous threat to our way of life since the Luftwaffe made its
15 energetic contribution to British town and country planning in 1940. Thousands

of green acres will be choked by concrete, as rapacious housebuilders devour whole landscapes. England's cherished green belts—the 14 great rings of protected fields that have stopped our major cities from sprawling outward for more than half a century—will be swept away.

20 Yet if you sweep away the apoplectic froth and the self-interested posturing and look at the reality, the "threat to the countryside" recedes dramatically. Yes, we do occupy a crowded little island. But what makes it seem crowded is that 98 per cent of us live on 7 per cent of the land. Britain is still overwhelmingly green. Just 11 per cent of our nation is classified as urban.

25 Moreover, planners reckon that as much as a quarter of the green belt around London is wasteland, largely devoid of landscape beauty. So why not use it to relieve the intolerable pressure on affordable housing in the capital? Because that would contravene the long-held myth that green belts are vital "lungs" for cities. Well, lungs they might be. But they benefit chiefly those who live in nice houses 30 inside the green belts (not least by keeping their property values sky-high); and then those who live in nice houses in the leafy outer suburbs; and not at all the people who need the fresh air most: those on inner-city estates.

The green-belt protectionists claim to be saving unspoilt countryside from the rampant advance of bulldozers. Exactly what unspoilt countryside do they imagine 35 they are saving? Primordial forest, unchanged since Boadicea thrashed the Romans? Hogwash. The English have been making and remaking their landscape for millennia to suit the needs of each passing generation.

These protectionists are fond of deriding any housebuilding targets set by the Government as monstrous, Soviet-style diktats. Good grief, what on earth do they 40 imagine that the planning laws protecting green belts and agricultural land are, if not Government interventions that have had a huge, and often disastrous, impact not just on the property market, but on employment, on transport, on public services and on economic growth?

And, of course, on homelessness. Every time a bunch of middle-class homeowners 45 fights off the "intrusion" of a new housing estate into their cherished landscape, they make it more difficult for the young and the poor to find somewhere to live in reasonable proximity to where they can find work. This is the 21st-century equivalent of pulling up the drawbridge after one's own family and friends are safely inside the castle.

[END OF TEXT]

X115/302

NATIONAL
QUALIFICATIONS
2008

THURSDAY, 15 MAY
9.00 AM – 10.30 AM

ENGLISH
HIGHER
Close Reading–Questions

Answer all questions. **Use your own words whenever possible and particularly when you are instructed to do so.**

50 marks are allocated to this paper.

A code letter (U, A, E) is used alongside each question to give some indication of the skills being assessed. The number of marks attached to each question will give some indication of the length of answer required.

Questions on Passage 1

Marks Code

1. Read lines 1–7.

   Explain in your own words why the writer seems surprised that there is so much coverage of the "countryside debate". (line 1)

   2 U

2. (*a*) Show how the word choice **and** sentence structure in lines 8–14 emphasise the strong feelings of those who feel the countryside is under threat.

   4 A

   (*b*) Show how the writer's use of language in lines 15–20 conveys his disapproval of the "action groups".

   2 A

3. Read lines 21–29.

   (*a*) By referring to specific words or phrases, show how lines 21–24 perform a linking function at this stage in the writer's argument.

   2 U

   (*b*) Referring to lines 25–29, explain in your own words what the writer believes to be a "particularly worrying aspect of the new rural mania" (line 23).

   2 U

4. "This view is palpably nonsensical." (lines 32–33)

   (*a*) Explain, using your own words as far as possible, what "this view" is. Refer to lines 30–32 in your answer.

   2 U

   (*b*) Give in your own words **one** of the writer's reasons in lines 33–38 (". . . ideas.") for believing that the view is "palpably nonsensical".

   2 U

   (*c*) Show how the writer's use of language in lines 38–41 reinforces his criticism of the conservationists' ideas.

   2 A

5. Read lines 42–53.

   Give, in your own words as far as possible, any **three** reasons why it is difficult to define the "traditional" British landscape.

   3 U

6. "This presented a serious challenge to Stone Age man . . ." (lines 58–59)

   (*a*) Explain in your own words what the "challenge" was. Refer to lines 54–61 (". . . trees.") in your answer.

   2 U

   (*b*) Explain in your own words how Stone Age man responded to the challenge. Refer to lines 61–69 in your answer.

   2 U

   (25)

Questions on Passage 2   *Marks   Code*

7. (*a*) By referring to lines 1–3, explain in your own words why the writer believes that the English middle classes are being "hypocritical".   2   U

   (*b*) Show how the writer's use of language in lines 4–10 creates a self-mocking tone.   2   A

8. Show how the writer's use of language in lines 11–19 emphasises the extreme nature of the English middle classes' view of the threat to the countryside.

   In your answer you should refer to specific language features such as: imagery, word choice, register . . .   4   A

9. Show how the writer's sentence structure **or** word choice in lines 20–24 emphasises his view that the threat to the countryside is much less serious than the English middle classes suggest.   2   A

10. (*a*) According to lines 25–27, why does the writer believe "a quarter of the green belt around London" should be used for housing?   2   U

    (*b*) How does the writer's use of language in lines 27 ("Because . . .") –32 cast doubt on the belief that green belts benefit everyone?   2   A

11. In lines 33–43 the writer criticises two further arguments put forward by the "green-belt protectionists".

    Choose **either** the argument discussed in lines 33–37 **or** the argument discussed in lines 38–43, and answer **both** of the following questions on the paragraph you have chosen.

    (*a*) Explain why, in the writer's opinion, the green-belt protectionists' argument is flawed.   2   U

    (*b*) How effective do you find the writer's use of language in conveying his attitude to their argument?   2   A/E

12. How effective do you find lines 44–49 as a conclusion to the writer's attack on the attitudes of "middle-class homeowners"?   2   E

                                                                        (20)

Question on both Passages

13. In Passage 1 David Sinclair refers to the claims of conservationists as "palpably nonsensical" and in Passage 2 Richard Morrison states that their views are "hogwash". Which writer is more successful in convincing you that these conservationists' claims are seriously flawed?

    Justify your choice by referring to the **ideas and/or style** of **both passages**.   5   E

                                                                        (5)

                                                        Total (50)

[END OF QUESTION PAPER]

[BLANK PAGE]

X115/303

NATIONAL
QUALIFICATIONS
2008

THURSDAY, 15 MAY
10.50 AM – 12.20 PM

ENGLISH
HIGHER
Critical Essay

Answer **two** questions.

Each question must be taken from a different section.

Each question is worth 25 marks.

Answer TWO questions from this paper. Each question must be chosen from a different Section (A–E). You are not allowed to choose two questions from the same Section.

In all Sections you may use Scottish texts.

Write the number of each question in the margin of your answer booklet and begin each essay on a fresh page.

You should spend about 45 minutes on each essay.

The following will be assessed:

- the relevance of your essays to the questions you have chosen, and the extent to which you sustain an appropriate line of thought

- your knowledge and understanding of key elements, central concerns and significant details of the chosen texts, supported by detailed and relevant evidence

- your understanding, as appropriate to the questions chosen, of how relevant aspects of structure/style/language contribute to the meaning/effect/impact of the chosen texts, supported by detailed and relevant evidence

- your evaluation, as appropriate to the questions chosen, of the effectiveness of the chosen texts, supported by detailed and relevant evidence

- the quality of your written expression and the technical accuracy of your writing.

SECTION A—DRAMA

Answers to questions on drama should address relevantly the central concern(s)/theme(s) of the text and be supported by reference to appropriate dramatic techniques such as: conflict, characterisation, key scene(s), dialogue, climax, exposition, dénouement, structure, plot, setting, aspects of staging (such as lighting, music, stage set, stage directions . . .), soliloquy, monologue . . .

1. Choose a play in which a central character is heroic yet vulnerable.

   Show how the dramatist makes you aware of both qualities and discuss how they affect your response to the character's fate in the play as a whole.

2. Choose a play which explores the theme of love in difficult circumstances.

   Explain how the dramatist introduces the theme and discuss how in the course of the play he/she prepares you for the resolution of the drama.

3. Choose from a play a scene in which an important truth is revealed.

   Briefly explain what the important truth is and assess the significance of its revelation to your understanding of theme or character.

4. Choose a play in which a character has to exist in a hostile environment.

   Briefly describe the environment and discuss the extent to which it influences your response to the character's behaviour and to the outcome of the play.

SECTION B—PROSE

Prose Fiction

> *Answers to questions on prose fiction should address relevantly the central concern(s)/theme(s) of the text(s) and be supported by reference to appropriate techniques of prose fiction such as: characterisation, setting, key incident(s), narrative technique, symbolism, structure, climax, plot, atmosphere, dialogue, imagery . . .*

5. Choose a **novel** which explores the cruelty of human nature.

   Show how the writer explores this theme and discuss how its exploration enhances your appreciation of the novel as a whole.

6. Choose a **novel** in which a confrontation between two characters is of central importance in the text.

   Explain the circumstances of the confrontation and discuss its importance to your understanding of the novel as a whole.

7. Choose **two short stories** which you appreciated because of the surprising nature of their endings.

   Compare the techniques used in creating these surprising endings and discuss which ending you feel is more successful as a conclusion.

8. Choose a **novel** or **short story** which is set during a period of social or political change.

   Discuss how important the writer's evocation of the period is to your appreciation of the text as a whole.

Prose Non-fiction

> *Answers to questions on prose non-fiction should address relevantly the central concern(s)/theme(s) of the text and be supported by reference to appropriate techniques of prose non-fiction such as: ideas, use of evidence, selection of detail, point of view, stance, setting, anecdote, narrative voice, style, language, structure, organisation of material . . .*

9. Choose a **non-fiction text** which you consider inspiring or provocative.

   Explain how the writer's presentation of his/her subject has such an impact on you.

10. Choose a piece of **travel writing** which offers surprising or amusing insights into a particular country or culture.

    Explain briefly what you learn about the country or culture and in greater detail discuss the techniques the writer uses to surprise or amuse you.

11. Choose a **non-fiction text** in which you consider the writer's stance on a particular issue to be ambiguous.

    Show how the writer's presentation of this issue illustrates the ambiguity of her/his stance.

[Turn over

SECTION C—POETRY

Answers to questions on poetry should address relevantly the central concern(s)/theme(s) of the text(s) and be supported by reference to appropriate poetic techniques such as: imagery, verse form, structure, mood, tone, sound, rhythm, rhyme, characterisation, contrast, setting, symbolism, word choice . . .

12. Choose a poem which deals with conflict or danger or death.

     Show how the poet creates an appropriate mood for the subject matter and go on to discuss how effectively she/he uses this mood to enhance your understanding of the central idea of the poem.

13. Choose a poem which is strongly linked to a specific location.

     Show how the poet captures the essence of the location and exploits this to explore an important theme.

14. Choose **two** poems which explore human relationships.

     By referring to both poems, discuss which you consider to be the more convincing portrayal of a relationship.

15. Choose a poem in which the speaker's personality is gradually revealed.

     Show how, through the content and language of the poem, aspects of the character gradually emerge.

SECTION D—FILM AND TV DRAMA

> *Answers to questions on film and TV drama should address relevantly the central concern(s)/theme(s) of the text(s) and be supported by reference to appropriate techniques of film and TV drama such as: key sequence(s), characterisation, conflict, structure, plot, dialogue, editing/montage, sound/soundtrack, aspects of mise-en-scène (such as lighting, colour, use of camera, costume, props . . .), mood, setting, casting, exploitation of genre . . .*

16. Choose a **film** or **TV drama*** in which a particular sequence is crucial to your understanding of an important theme.

    By referring to the sequence and to the text as a whole, show why you consider the sequence to be so important to your understanding of the theme.

17. Choose a **film** or **TV drama*** which presents a life-affirming story.

    By referring to key elements of the text, show how the story has such an effect.

18. Choose a **film** or **TV drama*** in which intense feelings have tragic consequences.

    Show to what extent the film or programme makers' presentation of these feelings and their consequences is successful in engaging you with the text.

19. Choose a **film** or **TV drama*** in which a complex character is revealed.

    Show how the film or programme makers reveal the complexity and discuss to what extent this aspect of the character contributes to your response to the text.

*"TV drama" includes a single play, a series or a serial.

[Turn over

SECTION E—LANGUAGE

Answers to questions on language should address relevantly the central concern(s) of the language research/study and be supported by reference to appropriate language concepts such as: register, jargon, tone, vocabulary, word choice, technical terminology, presentation, illustration, accent, grammar, idiom, slang, dialect, structure, point of view, orthography, abbreviation . . .

20. Consider uses of language designed to interest you in a social or commercial or political campaign.

    Identify aspects of language which you feel are intended to influence you and evaluate their success in raising your awareness of the subject of the campaign.

21. Consider the spoken language of a clearly defined group of people.

    Identify features which differentiate this language from standard usage and assess the extent to which these features have useful functions within the group.

22. Consider the language of newspaper reporting on such subjects as fashion, celebrities, reality TV, soap stars. . .

    Identify some of the characteristics of this language and discuss to what extent it is effective in communicating with its target audience.

23. Consider the language (written and/or symbolic) associated with the use of e-mails or text messaging or instant messaging.

    Describe some of the conventions associated with any one of these and discuss to what extent these conventions lead to more effective communication.

[END OF QUESTION PAPER]

2009

[BLANK PAGE]

X115/301

NATIONAL
QUALIFICATIONS
2009

FRIDAY, 15 MAY
9.00 AM – 10.45 AM

ENGLISH
HIGHER
Close Reading—Text

There are TWO passages and questions.

Read the passages carefully and then answer all the questions, which are printed in a separate booklet.

You should read the passages to:

understand what the writers are saying about issues surrounding our use of natural resources (**Understanding—U**);

analyse their choices of language, imagery and structures to recognise how they convey their points of view and contribute to the impact of the passage (**Analysis—A**);

evaluate how effectively they have achieved their purpose (**Evaluation—E**).

PASSAGE 1

The first passage is from an article in The Telegraph *newspaper in January 2007. In it, Janet Daley responds to suggestions that we should limit our use of natural resources.*

A DOOMSDAY SCENARIO?

Is your journey really necessary? Who would have thought that, in the absence of world war and in the midst of unprecedented prosperity, politicians would be telling us not to travel? Just as working people have begun to enjoy the freedoms that the better-off have known for generations—the experience of other cultures, other

5 cuisines, other climates—they are threatened with having those liberating possibilities priced out of their reach.

And when I hear politicians—most of them comfortably off—trying to deny enlightenment and pleasure to "working class" people, I reach for my megaphone. Maybe Tommy Tattoo and his mates do use cheap flights to the sunshine as an

10 extension of their binge-drinking opportunities, but for thousands of people whose parents would never have ventured beyond Blackpool or Rothesay, air travel has been a social revelation.

So, before we all give the eco-lobby's anti-flying agenda the unconditional benefit of the doubt, can we just review their strategy as a whole?

15 Remember, it is not just air travel that the green tax lobby is trying to control: it is a restriction on any mobility. Clamping down on one form of movement, as the glib reformers have discovered, simply creates intolerable pressure on the others. Londoners, for example, had just become accustomed to the idea that they would have to pay an £8 congestion charge to drive into their own city when they

20 discovered that the fares on commuter rail and underground services had been hiked up with the intention of driving away customers from the public transport system—now grossly overcrowded as a result of people having been forced off the roads by the congestion charge.

The only solution—and I am just waiting for the politicians to recommend it

25 explicitly—is for none of us to go anywhere. Stay at home and save the planet. But that would be a craven retreat from all the social, professional and cultural interactions that unrestricted mobility makes possible—and which, since the Renaissance, have made great cities the centres of intellectual progress.

Even devising a way of making a living while never leaving your house would not

30 absolve you of your ecological guilt, because you'd still be making liberal use of the technology that has transformed domestic life. The working classes, having only discovered in the last generation or two the comforts of a tolerable degree of warmth and plentiful hot water, are now being told that these things must be rationed or prohibitively taxed.

35 Never mind that the universal presence of adequate heating has almost eliminated those perennial scourges of the poor—bronchitis and pneumonia—which once took the very young and the very old in huge numbers every winter. Never mind that the generous use of hot water and detergent, particularly when combined in a washing machine for the laundering of bed linen and clothing, has virtually eliminated the

40 infestations of body lice and fleas (which once carried plague) that used to be a commonplace feature of poverty. Never mind that the private car, the Green Public Enemy Number One, has given ordinary families freedom and flexibility that would have been inconceivable in previous generations.

If politicians are planning restrictions on these "polluting" aspects of private life, to
45 be enforced by a price mechanism, they had better accept that they will be
reconstructing a class divide that will drastically affect the quality of life of those on
the wrong side of it.

It is certainly possible that the premises advanced by environmental campaigners are
sound: that we are in mortal danger from global warming and that this is a result of
50 human activity. Yet when I listen to ecological warnings such as these, I am
reminded of a doomsday scenario from the past.

In his *Essay on the Principle of Population*, published in 1798, Thomas Malthus
demonstrated, in what appeared to be indisputable mathematical terms, that
population growth would exceed the limits of food supply by the middle of the 19th
55 century. Only plague, war or natural disaster would be capable of sufficiently
reducing the numbers of people to avert mass starvation within roughly 50 years.
This account of the world's inevitable fate (known as the "Malthusian catastrophe")
was as much part of accepted thinking among intellectuals then as are the
environmental lobby's warnings today.

60 Malthus, however, had made a critical conceptual mistake: he underestimated the
complexity of human behaviour. Population did not go on increasing at the same
rate; it responded to economic and social conditions. Moreover, he had discounted
the force of ingenuity in finding ways to increase food supply. In actual fact, the
introduction of intensive farming methods and the invention of pesticides
65 transformed what he had assumed would be the simple, fixed relation between
numbers of people and amount of resource. He had made what seemed to be a
sound prediction without allowing for the possibility that inventiveness and
innovation might alter the picture in unimaginable ways.

Warnings of catastrophe come and go. Whatever their validity, we cannot and
70 should not ask people to go back to a more restricted way of life. The restrictions
would not work anyway, because they are impracticable. If they were enforced, they
would be grotesquely unfair and socially divisive. If we really are facing an
environmental crisis, then we are going to have to innovate and engineer our way out
of it.

PASSAGE 2

Leo Hickman, writing in The Guardian *newspaper in May 2006, explores the ethics of leisure-related flights.*

IS IT OK TO FLY?

I am desperate for some good news about aviation and its environmental impact.
Please someone say that they got the figures wrong. I have always loved the
freedom and access flying brings—who doesn't?—but in recent years I have
descended into near-permanent depression about how to square this urge with the
5 role of at least trying to be a responsible citizen of the planet. Travel is one of life's
pleasures, but is my future—and, more importantly, that of my two young
daughters—really going to be one of abstinence from flying, or at best flying by
quota, as many environmentalists are now calling for?

I recently travelled to Geneva to attend the second "Aviation and Environment
10 Summit" in search of, if not answers, then at least a better indication of just how
damaging flying really is to the environment. (The irony was not lost that hundreds
of people had flown from around the world to attend.)

Speaker after speaker bemoaned how the public had somehow misunderstood the
aviation industry and had come to believe that aviation is a huge and
15 disproportionate polluter. Let's get this in perspective, said repeated speakers: this
is small fry compared with cars, factories, even homes. Why are we being singled
out, they cried? Why not, they said, chase after other industries that could easily
make efficiency savings instead of picking on an industry that gives so much to the
world, yet is currently so economically fragile?

20 But even in this self-interested arena a representative from the US Federal Aviation
Administration caused some sharp intakes of breath from the audience by showing
an extraordinary map of current flightpaths etched over one another on the world's
surface. The only places on Earth that are not scarred by routes are blocks of air
space over the central Pacific, the southern Atlantic and Antarctica.

25 It seems, therefore, that we who avidly consume cheap flights do indeed have to face
a choice. Do we continue to take our minibreaks, visit our second homes, holiday on
the other side of the world and partake of all the other forms of what the industry
describes as "non-essential" travel? Or do we start to ration this habit, even if
others elsewhere in the world quite understandably will be quick to take our place
30 on the plane? My view is that flying will simply have to become more expensive.
Only by becoming more expensive will ticket prices start to reflect more closely the
environmental impact of flying—the polluter should always pay, after all—and
therefore drive down demand. It's easy to forget how good we've had it in this
heady era of low-cost carriers—but surely the good times must end.

35 A remedy such as carbon-neutralising our flights is a nice, cuddly idea that on the
surface is a positive action to take, but planting trees in Thailand or handing out
eco-lightbulbs in Honduras is no substitute for getting planes out of the skies. It
also carries the risk that people will think "job done" and simply carry on flying
regardless.

[END OF TEXT]

X115/302

NATIONAL QUALIFICATIONS 2009	FRIDAY, 15 MAY 9.00 AM – 10.45 AM	ENGLISH HIGHER Close Reading–Questions

Answer all questions. **Use your own words whenever possible and particularly when you are instructed to do so.**

50 marks are allocated to this paper.

A code letter (U, A, E) is used alongside each question to give some indication of the skills being assessed. The number of marks attached to each question will give some indication of the length of answer required.

Questions on Passage 1

Marks   Cod

1. (*a*) Referring to lines 1–6, give in your own words **two** reasons why the writer finds it surprising that politicians are "telling us not to travel".   2   U

   (*b*) Show how the writer's sentence structure **and** word choice in lines 1–12 convey the strength of her commitment to air travel for all.   4   A

2. Referring to specific words and/or phrases, show how the sentence "So, before . . . as a whole?" (lines 13–14) performs a linking function in the writer's argument.   2   U

3. Read lines 15–23.

   (*a*) What, according to the writer, is the result of "Clamping down on one form of movement"? Use your own words in your answer.   1   U

   (*b*) Explain how the writer uses the example of the London congestion charge to demonstrate her point.   2   U

4. In the paragraph from lines 24 to 28, the writer states that "The only solution . . . is for none of us to go anywhere." (lines 24–25)

   (*a*) Why, according to the writer, is this "solution" undesirable?   2   U

   (*b*) Show how, in this paragraph, the writer creates a tone which conveys her disapproval of the "solution".   2   A

5. Read lines 29–47.

   (*a*) Why, according to the writer, would "never leaving your house" still involve some "ecological guilt"?   1   U

   (*b*) Using your own words as far as possible, summarise the benefits of technology as described in lines 35–43.   3   U

   (*c*) Show how the writer uses sentence structure in lines 35–43 to strengthen her argument.   2   A

   (*d*) What, according to the writer in lines 44–47, would be the outcome of the restrictions proposed by politicians?   2   U

6. Read lines 48–68.

   (*a*) What does the phrase "doomsday scenario" (line 51) mean?   1   U

   (*b*) In your own words, outline the "doomsday scenario" predicted by Thomas Malthus.   2   U

   (*c*) In your own words, give any **two** reasons why Malthus's theory proved incorrect.   2   U

7. How effective do you find the writer's use of language in the final paragraph (lines 69–74) in emphasising her opposition to placing restrictions on people's way of life?   2   A/E

                                                     (30)

Questions on Passage 2   *Marks Code*

8. (*a*) Explain the cause of the writer's "depression" (line 4).   2   U

   (*b*) Show how the writer's use of language in lines 1–8 creates an emotional
       appeal to the reader.   2   A

9. Read lines 9–24.

   (*a*) Explain the "irony" referred to in line 11.   1   U

   (*b*) Show how the writer's use of language in lines 13–19 conveys his
       unsympathetic view of the speakers at the conference. In your answer
       you should refer to at least **two** features such as sentence structure, tone,
       word choice . . .   4   A

   (*c*) How effective do you find the writer's use of imagery in lines 20–24 in
       conveying the impact that flying has on the environment?   2   A/E

10. Explain why the writer believes that "flying will simply have to become more
     expensive" (line 30).   2   U

11. Show how the writer, in lines 35–39, creates a dismissive tone when discussing
     possible remedies.   2   A

                                                                       (15)

Question on both Passages

12. Which passage is more effective in engaging your interest in aspects of the
     environmental debate?

     Justify your choice by referring to the **ideas and style** of **both passages**.   5   E

                                                                       (5)

                                                        Total (50)

[END OF QUESTION PAPER]

[BLANK PAGE]

X115/303

NATIONAL
QUALIFICATIONS
2009

FRIDAY, 15 MAY
11.05 AM – 12.35 PM

ENGLISH
HIGHER
Critical Essay

Answer **two** questions.

Each question must be taken from a different section.

Each question is worth 25 marks.

Answer TWO questions from this paper. Each question must be chosen from a different Section (A–E). You are not allowed to choose two questions from the same Section.

In all Sections you may use Scottish texts.

Write the number of each question in the margin of your answer booklet and begin each essay on a fresh page.

You should spend about 45 minutes on each essay.

The following will be assessed:

- the relevance of your essays to the questions you have chosen, and the extent to which you sustain an appropriate line of thought

- your knowledge and understanding of key elements, central concerns and significant details of the chosen texts, supported by detailed and relevant evidence

- your understanding, as appropriate to the questions chosen, of how relevant aspects of structure/style/language contribute to the meaning/effect/impact of the chosen texts, supported by detailed and relevant evidence

- your evaluation, as appropriate to the questions chosen, of the effectiveness of the chosen texts, supported by detailed and relevant evidence

- the quality of your written expression and the technical accuracy of your writing.

SECTION A—DRAMA

Answers to questions on drama should address relevantly the central concern(s)/theme(s) of the text and be supported by reference to appropriate dramatic techniques such as: conflict, characterisation, key scene(s), dialogue, climax, exposition, dénouement, structure, plot, setting, aspects of staging (such as lighting, music, stage set, stage directions . . .), soliloquy, monologue . . .

1. Choose a play in which a central character behaves in an obsessive manner.

    Describe the nature of the character's obsessive behaviour and discuss the influence this behaviour has on your understanding of the character in the play as a whole.

2. Choose a play which you feel is made particularly effective by features of structure such as: dramatic opening, exposition, flashback, contrast, turning-point, climax, anticlimax, dénouement . . .

    Show how one or more than one structural feature employed by the dramatist adds to the impact of the play.

3. Choose from a play a scene which significantly changes your view of a character.

    Explain how the scene prompts this reappraisal and discuss how important it is to your understanding of the character in the play as a whole.

4. Choose a play set in a society whose values conflict with those of a central character or characters.

    Describe this difference in values and discuss how effectively the opposition of values enhances your appreciation of the play as a whole.

SECTION B—PROSE

Prose Fiction

> *Answers to questions on prose fiction should address relevantly the central concern(s)/theme(s) of the text(s) and be supported by reference to appropriate techniques of prose fiction such as: characterisation, setting, key incident(s), narrative technique, symbolism, structure, climax, plot, atmosphere, dialogue, imagery . . .*

5. Choose a **novel** or **short story** which deals with true love, unrequited love or love betrayed.

   Discuss the writer's exploration of the theme and show to what extent it conveys a powerful message about the nature of love.

6. Choose a **novel** or **short story** with a central character you consider to be heroic.

   Show how the heroic qualities are revealed and discuss how this portrayal of the character enhances your understanding of the text as a whole.

7. Choose a **novel** in which the setting in time and/or place is a significant feature.

   Show how the writer's use of setting contributes to your understanding of character and theme.

8. Choose a **novel** in which there is an incident involving envy or rivalry or distrust.

   Explain the nature of the incident and go on to discuss its importance to your understanding of the novel as a whole.

Prose Non-fiction

> *Answers to questions on prose non-fiction should address relevantly the central concern(s)/theme(s) of the text and be supported by reference to appropriate techniques of prose non-fiction such as: ideas, use of evidence, selection of detail, point of view, stance, setting, anecdote, narrative voice, style, language, structure, organisation of material . . .*

9. Choose an **essay** or a **piece of journalism** in which you feel that the writer's style is a key factor in developing a persuasive argument.

   Show how the writer's presentation of the argument is made persuasive by his or her use of techniques of non-fiction.

10. Choose a **full-length work** of **biography** or of **autobiography** in which the writer presents the life of her or his subject in a positive light.

    Show how the writer's style and skilful selection of material contribute to this positive portrayal.

11. Choose a **non-fiction text** which exploits the humour of particular situations and/or incidents.

    Show how the writer's use of humour creates interest in the subject matter.

SECTION C—POETRY

Answers to questions on poetry should address relevantly the central concern(s)/theme(s) of the text(s) and be supported by reference to appropriate poetic techniques such as: imagery, verse form, structure, mood, tone, sound, rhythm, rhyme, characterisation, contrast, setting, symbolism, word choice . . .

12. Choose a poem in which the poet explores one of the following emotions: anguish, dissatisfaction, regret, loss.

    Show how the poet explores the emotion and discuss to what extent he or she is successful in deepening your understanding of it.

13. Choose **two** poems which explore the experience of war.

    Discuss which you find more effective in conveying the experience of war.

14. Choose a poem in which contrast is important in developing theme.

    Explore the poet's use of contrast and show why it is important in developing a key theme of the poem.

15. Choose a poem which depicts a particular stage of life, such as childhood, adolescence, middle age, old age.

    Discuss how effectively the poet evokes the essence of this stage of life.

SECTION D—FILM AND TV DRAMA

> *Answers to questions on film and TV drama should address relevantly the central concern(s)/theme(s) of the text(s) and be supported by reference to appropriate techniques of film and TV drama such as: key sequence(s), characterisation, conflict, structure, plot, dialogue, editing/montage, sound/soundtrack, aspects of mise-en-scène (such as lighting, colour, use of camera, costume, props . . .), mood, setting, casting, exploitation of genre . . .*

16. Choose a **film** or **TV drama*** in which two characters are involved in a psychological conflict which dominates the text.

Show how the film or programme makers reveal the nature of the conflict and explain why it is so significant to the text as a whole.

17. Choose from a **film** an important sequence in which excitement is created as much by filmic technique as by action and dialogue.

Show how the film makers create this excitement and explain why the sequence is so important to the film as a whole.

18. Choose a **film** or **TV drama*** which evokes a particular period of history and explores significant concerns of life at that time.

By referring to selected sequences and to the text as a whole, show how the film or programme makers evoke the period and explore significant concerns of life at that time.

19. Choose one or more than one **film** which in your opinion demonstrate(s) outstanding work by a particular director.

By referring to key elements of the text(s), show why you consider the work of this director to be so impressive.

*"TV drama" includes a single play, a series or a serial.

[Turn over

SECTION E—LANGUAGE

> *Answers to questions on language should address relevantly the central concern(s) of the language research/study and be supported by reference to appropriate language concepts such as: register, jargon, tone, vocabulary, word choice, technical terminology, presentation, illustration, accent, grammar, idiom, slang, dialect, structure, point of view, orthography, abbreviation . . .*

20. Consider aspects of language which change over time, such as slang, idiom, dialect . . .

Identify some of the changes and discuss to what extent you feel these changes contribute towards possible problems in communication between different age groups or generations.

21. Consider some of the changes in language which have occurred as a result of lobbying by pressure groups such as feminists, multi-cultural organisations, faith groups . . .

By examining specific examples, discuss to what extent you feel that clarity of communication has been affected by such changes.

22. Consider the use of persuasive language in the promotion of goods or services or a campaign or a cause.

By examining specific examples, evaluate the success of the language in achieving its purpose.

23. Consider the technical language associated with a sport, a craft, a profession or one of the arts.

By examining specific examples, discuss to what extent you feel such language leads to clearer communication.

[END OF QUESTION PAPER]

[BLANK PAGE]

[BLANK PAGE]

[BLANK PAGE]

[BLANK PAGE]

[BLANK PAGE]

Acknowledgements

Permission has been sought from all relevant copyright holders and Bright Red Publishing is grateful for the use of the following:

The article 'The Shape of Things to Come' from www.economist.com, 11 December 2003 © The Economist Newspaper Limited, London 2003 (2006 Close Reading pages 2 & 3);

The article 'Foolish Panic is About Profit' by Susie Orbach, taken from The Observer, 30 May 2004. Reproduced by permission of Susie Orbach. (2006 Close Reading page 4);

An article adapted from 'Despite Google, we still need good libraries' by George Kerevan, taken from The Scotsman, 15 December 2004 © The Scotsman Publications Ltd. (2007 Close Reading pages 2 & 3);

The article 'Paradise is Paper, Vellum and Dust' by Ben Macintyre © The Times/NI Syndication, 18 December 2004 (2007 Close Reading pages 3 & 4);

Adapted extract taken from 'Shades of Green' by David Sinclair. Published by Grafton Books (Harper Collins). Reproduced with permission of David Sinclair (2008 Close Reading pages 2 & 3);

The article 'Yes, I will let Mr Prescott build in my backyard' by Richard Morrison © The Times/NI Syndication, 30 April 2004 (2008 Close Reading pages 3 & 4);

The article 'If Eco-Snobs had their way, none of us would go anywhere', by Janet Daley taken from The Telegraph © Telegraph Media Group Limited (8 January 2007) (2009 Close Reading pages 2 & 3);

The article 'Is it OK to fly?' by Leo Hickman, 20 May 2006. Copyright Guardian News & Media Ltd 2006 (2009 Close Reading pages 3 & 4).